Local Success and Federal Failure

Local Success and Federal Failure: A Study of Community Development and Educational Change in the Rural South

CHARLES A. CLINTON
Mississippi State University

ABT BOOKS
CAMBRIDGE, MASSACHUSETTS

Library of Congress Catalog Card Number 79-55667

Printed in the United States of America.

ISBN: 0-89011-538-9

Contents

Foreword

As our knowledge of American communities has grown steadily over the years, we have become alerted to the importance of ties which bind local units to the greater society. The impression is that these vertical ties are multiplying and growing stronger in ways that threaten the very existence of local units. Indeed, one imagines a giant, urban, cultural centrifuge at the heart of society, ceaselessly reaching for the small community, making it at once vulnerable and dependent.

Local Success and Federal Failure adds to our understanding of American community life but not in the conventional sense. It makes no effort to describe all aspects of the life of a community; rather, it hones in on the politics of planned change. Through the sensitive eyes of Dr. Clinton we thus become privy in a very personal way to how the people of Shiloh choose their future. It is not surprising to learn that in this rural county individual and collective decisions about change emerge from the mix of kin, neighbor, church, and community loyalties. Nor is it surprising to sense that the people of Shiloh enjoy manipulating these networks as they compete for the location of school and courthouse and the distribution of county road funds, influence the hiring and firing of teachers, and express their concern for a host of other local issues which bear on personal ends.

Our glimpse into Shiloh differs from that into many of the other small communities described by anthropologists. Here we move from an account of how local issues are decided to an understanding of how extralocal issues are made local and then dealt with in conventional Shiloh ways. The image that emerges is not that of a community buffeted by outside influences but rather of one that is very much in control. Put another way, in this account we learn how the people of Shiloh outmanipulate the manipulators. This is grassroots politics laid bare.

During the 1960s Shiloh County floated municipal industrial bonds – some $200 million worth – to attract industry. When industrial development exacerbated conditions in the schools, the county turned again to external sources for the solution to local problems. This time, however, the approach was more sophisticated: professional consultants were hired to help draft the proposal that enabled Shiloh to become one of ten rural school systems participating in an experimental program sponsored by the U.S. Department of Education.

Local Success and Federal Failure evaluates the management and the fortunes of Shiloh's Experimental Schools program as it runs up against concern for local autonomy. The central issue dealt with here – effecting change in a pluralistic society – is one that ought to command more explicit attention by social scientists. Dr. Clinton's analysis calls attention to the strengths of local culture when its carriers are properly motivated to control process. On the practical side, this local strength may occasionally result in a standoff between the community and the representatives of central power. When this happens, as it did in Shiloh, the outsiders who lay claim to power over local decisions sometimes find the roles reversed – they become dependent on local units for whatever measure of success they manage. On the theoretical side, our understanding of how the strength of local culture is tapped, as it is in Shiloh, provides some insight into how culture persists, and especially into the process of reintegration which culture seems constantly to experience.

Shiloh's success may not be typical of the extent to which a local community can manipulate the external environment. To the extent that it has been successful, however, Shiloh is a case worthy of our attention.

Art Gallaher, Jr.

August 1979
Lexington, Kentucky

Preface

This ethnographic account of developmental change in Shiloh County (a pseudonym for a small, rural political subdivision of the American South) focuses on the processes of political decision making, particularly where those processes have led to choices altering the course and velocity of planned change.

My presence as a professional ethnographer in Shiloh County resulted from the local decision that the Shiloh County Public School System would participate in the federal government's Experimental Schools Program. Administered by the National Institute of Education, the program was based on the principle of fostering comprehensive changes in education by funding locally initiated improvements and innovations. As part of the effort to evaluate this unique federal program, I agreed to live in Shiloh County for three and one-half years; to help gather data for various quantitative studies; and to write both a history and an ethnography of Shiloh, its communities, and its educational system. There were no guidelines for the ethnography save that it be grounded in data and that it describe the county's participation in the Experimental Schools program – what happened and why.

My first task as a researcher was to find a focus to guide my empirical efforts. Shiloh itself provided an immediate solution to the problem of focus. Upon arriving in Shiloh County in April 1973,

I went to Cuba Landing's city hall in order to change the utilities account for my apartment from the name of the previous tenant to mine. At the time, the city hall was a brick building that had been used as a corner grocery store before being converted to public service. The building was in poor repair, too small to house the city's business, and adorned with the painted appellation of "Kangaroo Court" on the outside eastern wall. Taped to the cashier's window was an old newspaper clipping announcing that work had begun on a $50 million aluminum plant financed by the Cuba Landing City Council through the issuance of municipal industrial bonds. Just down the street was the partially finished, new city hall – a spacious, modern building financed by the revenue generated through industrialization.

I returned home. The view from my apartment window included Shiloh's consolidated high school. The building was old, in need of repair, too small for the number of students enrolled, and decorated with painted graffiti on the outside northern wall. Adjacent to the old high school was an impressively modern high school under construction. Further afield were the smoke stacks of a $150 million industrial facility whose construction was financed through the county government's issuance of municipal industrial bonds. A tax levied on these industries was helping to fund school construction.

Here was the solution to my problem of focus: the counties towns, governments, and schools were apparently making the political decisions to use external resources to meet local needs. As a result, Shiloh was forging an impressive record in the annals of developmental change.

The next task was to discover whether the linkages among town, county, and school development were real and intentional. It soon became obvious to me not only that the linkages were real, but also that Shiloh County was an exceptional rural community. Graduate training in anthropology had taught me the standard analysis of rural communities as groups of people in institutional constellations linked together through a sharing of personnel and values. Furthermore, my graduate studies assured me that local change was never due to local initiative, but rather was dependent upon external policies and decisions affecting local units. Yet the institutions within Shiloh were apparently manipulating external resources to meet locally defined needs in ways neither envisioned nor sanctioned by external policymakers. Shiloh's performance seemed to invite an ethnographic approach to the documentation and explanation of county decision making, an approach that I was eager to employ.

The places, events, and people described in this book are real, but Shiloh County, *The Shiloh Crier,* Cuba Landing, South Shiloh, Clarksville, Bill Wheeler, Tom Blaine, Frank Henry, Ray Bass, Bob Robbins, Fred Harold, Sam Collins, and all other names are pseudonyms. The teachers described in Shiloh's schools are real, but they have been stripped of identifying characteristics so that their individual actions and speeches cannot return to haunt them.

Not all that was learned in Shiloh has been reported. Some of the deletions are a clear loss because they would help clarify the way in which Shiloh frames the issues that call for decisions about people in leadership positions. But to disclose this information might cause some of Shiloh's citizens personal grief. While the aims and goals of ethnography are to lay bare the hold that life has on people, no high principle gives the ethnographer license to use his knowledge to harm people directly or to destroy reputations. In this ethnography, I have tried to honor that personal ethic.

Acknowledgments

While I am solely responsible for the substance of this volume, I have had a great deal of help in bringing Shiloh County's vitality into focus. The staff at the National Institute of Education, which sponsored my research, have been patient in waiting for me to bring the study into a readable form. Dr. Robert Herriott has been both director of the largest project with which I have been affiliated since 1973 and a source of skilled and patient help. Dr. Howard Becker proved to be an insightful reviewer of an earlier draft of this volume, ignoring what was not relevant and guiding me toward the matters of interest in Shiloh's record. Dr. Elizabeth Eddy has also been helpful, especially in her comments about the influence of community on schools. Dr. Stephen Fitzsimmons, Dr. Michael G. Trend, Dr. Manuel Carlos, Dr. Thomas Payzant, Ms. Mary E. Schumacher, Ms. Abby J. Freedman, and Dr. Robert Nakamura have all served as reviewers, and I appreciate their comments. Dr. Harry Wolcott has also contributed helpful advice.

This volume owes a special debt to Dr. Art Gallaher, Jr., who helped me with the developmental change framework and provided consistent insight during times when I was deluged with inconsistent counsel.

Of course, the people and leaders of Shiloh County aided my writing of this book from beginning to end. Had they not been willing to share their knowledge, thoughts, and feelings, this volume could never have taken shape. I hope that this account in some way makes them feel that their efforts on my behalf were worthwhile.

There is another group that deserves special thanks – my family. My wife Pat has endured my fascination with Shiloh County for five years. My daughter Laura has been without her father's company too many times because of *Project Rural.* And my daughter Catherine has grown from infant to child with a father whose attentions were all too often fixed upon Shiloh. It is now time to turn from all the experiences of the past five years and to begin introducing Catherine to the literature of childhood. Given the events witnessed in Shiloh, *The Little Engine that Could* seems like an appropriate beginning.

Mississippi State, Mississippi
November, 1978

Charles A. Clinton

Introduction

Introduction

The thesis of this book is that Shiloh County's record of institutional modification is the result of local decision making. While these choices involve using this or that external resource to satisfy local needs, the decisions are political responses to local demands for a better quality of life. To understand Shiloh's record is to understand the county, its social and cultural contexts, and the ways in which local leaders respond to the demands that these contexts generate. Shiloh's leaders use external resources to meet constituent demands. When these resources are not precisely aligned with constituent demands, Shiloh's political processes alter the resources to fit the local context. In this way the leaders can meet the needs of the county and further consolidate their hold on local sources of power and influence.

The conceptual framework for my thesis concerning local decision making in Shiloh County is drawn from an interdisciplinary perspective on developmental change in rural settings. Developmental change involves "social planning, but not merely of goals, but also of processes and strategies for attaining goals."[1] Shiloh's goal was that of institutional change; the county's strategies involved the use of external resources to meet local needs; the processes were political; and the analytical stance I have adopted derives from literature on developmental change from a variety of disciplines.

Shiloh's story – one which I tell by using primary and secondary data to illustrate the processes, decisions, and outcomes of the county's quest for developmental change – is marked by a series of successes. In contrast to the finding that industries tend to locate in urban rather than in rural areas,[2] Shiloh used federal tax codes and other inducements to attract nearly $300 million worth of industrial facilities between 1955 and 1968. And contrary to the finding that rural governments do not convert private sector growth into public sector revenue,[3] Shiloh invoked state laws to tax its new industry between 1970 and 1973. Finally, between 1970 and 1976 the county government and school system used a mixture of local funds and state and federal programs to improve facilities and services in the county.

Shiloh's successes are dramatic in view of the cases in which attempts to promote programs of developmental change have failed. Paddock sums up the failures of international efforts with the statement that "developmental professionals do not know how to carry out an effective economic program."[4] Paddock's assessment of international efforts is paralleled by evaluations of domestic programs. Charles L. Schultze, an economist with extensive policy-making experience, notes that, while the federal government has been committed to domestic policies of developmental change, "the history of the 1960's makes clear that current federal approaches are not effective."[5]

One reason programs of developmental change have had disappointing results is that they rely on the hypothesis that decisions made in the centers of power will have predictable impacts on local units. As an anthropologist phrases it, "Development in conventional theory and practice characteristically comes from above, externally imposed by governments or bureaucracies."[6] A political scientist phrases the impact hypothesis more sharply:

> The developmental strategies of governments, universities, business organizations, and other associations are the principal independent variables . . . . Different kinds of development – economic, social, political, technological – are the ultimate dependent variables.[7]

The impact hypothesis assumes that governments control the *systemic linkages* between themselves and local institutions and that *living links* are both responsive to governmental priorities and effective in implementing them locally.

Systemic linkages are defined as the connections between "one or more of the elements of at least two social systems . . . articulated in such a manner that the two systems in some ways and on some occasions may be viewed as a single unit."[8] To achieve systemic linkage while boundaries between the systems are being maintained, "the contacts may be made the responsibility of various institutionalized liaison status-roles in which the incumbents act as living links between the groups engaged in the exchange."[9]

Another anthropologist, John Bennett, has challenged both the impact hypothesis and the assumptions upon which it rests on the basis that they make no allowance for the workings of local political autonomy. Bennett reports several instances in which local initiative either stayed or reversed the impacts of developmental programs in Saskatchewan, Canada. Assumptions about the control of systemic linkages lead to a distorted view, Bennett argues, because they fail to account for "the fact that members of rural communities have *desired* closer contact with the urban-national society and culture," and that such communities have sometimes managed to "manipulate and control" external agencies.[10] Through local control of living links, governmental policy and bureaucratic programs have been modified to fit local contexts.[11] Thus, Bennett suggests that local political autonomy rather than the influence of external agencies may be responsible for developmental change in rural communities.

Shiloh's experience in achieving developmental change supports the local political autonomy hypothesis rather than the impact hypothesis. Shiloh was successful in its programs because it used local leaders as living links, people who were responsive to local needs rather than to priorities established by external agencies. These local people viewed national policy and federal and state programs as resources that could be harnessed to meet local demands for change. This exercise of local political autonomy had two outcomes: first, it ensured that Shiloh's programs of developmental change had community impacts; second, it further consolidated Shiloh's sources of power and influence into stable political bases. In those instances where programs of developmental change were imposed upon Shiloh, the county's political processes intervened to alter the anticipated course and velocity of change.

Shiloh's case has important implications for federal policy. After concluding that federal approaches to domestic programs of developmental change were not effective, Schultze et al. recommended that the federal government embark "on a program of social experimentation" to learn how to change local institutions.[12] The federally funded Experimental Schools program is one such experiment. As it happened, Shiloh's schools were in the process of meeting local demands for improved facilities and services when news of the Experimental Schools program arrived in the district. My account of educational change in Shiloh provides a context for evaluating not only two approaches to developmental change, but the utility of Schultze's policy recommendation as well.

These themes are explored in great depth throughout the remainder of this volume. Part One describes how familialism, religion, neighborhood, community, and the county itself provide communal frames of reference that command loyalties and are, in many cases, the substance of political decision making. Part One also illustrates differing communal responses to the two approaches to developmental change by showing that political decisions in some county agencies led to developmental changes, while an externally imposed program of change was altered by local political processes. Part Two moves from a general community context to that of educational affairs and shows how Shiloh's communal frames of reference supported educational changes that were justified as being in the county's best interests while altering imposed programs of developmental change. The final chapter synthesizes what has been learned about change and persistence in Shiloh. Here description gives way to an interdisciplinary analysis of the relationships between Shiloh's communal frames of reference and the county's systemic linkages with external agencies in an effort to assess the relative efficacy of the impact and local autonomy hypotheses for explaining both developmental change and the lack thereof.

Notes

1. Art Gallaher, Jr., "Developmental Change and the Social Sciences: Introduction," in *Perspectives on Developmental Change*, ed. Art Gallaher, Jr. (Lexington, Kentucky: University of Kentucky Press, 1968), p. 4.
2. David M. Smith, *Industrial Location: An Economic Geographical Analysis* (New York: John Wiley and Sons, 1971), p. 508.
3. Gene F. Summers, "Small Towns Beware: Industry can be Costly," *Planning* 42, no. 4 (1976): 20.

4. William and Elizabeth Paddock, *We Don't Know How* (Ames, Iowa: Iowa State University Press, 1973), p. 299.
5. Charles Schultze et al., *Setting National Priorities: The 1973 Budget* (Washington, D.C.: The Brookings Institution, 1972), p. 458.
6. David C. Pitt, *Development from Below: Anthropologists and Developmental Situations* (The Hague: Mouton Publishers, 1976), p. 4.
7. Edward Weidner, "Developmental Change and the Social Sciences: Conclusion," in *Perspectives on Developmental Change*, ed. Art Gallaher, Jr. (Lexington, Kentucky: University of Kentucky Press, 1968), pp. 231-56.
8. Charles P. Loomis, *Social Systems: Essays on their Persistence and Change* (Princeton, N.J.: D. Van Nostrand Company, 1960), p. 32.
9. Ibid., p. 33.
10. John W. Bennett, "Microcosm-Macrocosm Relationships in North American Agrarian Society," *American Anthropologist* 69 (1967): 442.
11. Ibid., pp. 446-448.
12. Schultze et al., *Setting National Priorities,* pp. 462-463.

CAST OF CHARACTERS

Cuba Landing

Bob Robbins	The mayor of Cuba Landing and leader of the Citizens' Ticket.
John Horn	A member of the Cuba Landing City Council, the leader of the Better Government for Cuba Landing Ticket, and Mr. Robbins's main opponent.
David Roe	The attorney for the Cuba Landing City Council.

Clarksville

Fred Harold	The mayor of Clarksville and the leader of the Progressive Ticket.
George Chesney	Twice a member of the Clarksville City Council, the leader of the Citizen's Ticket, and Harold's main opponent in election campaigns.

The Court House

Ray Bass	Republican county judge for Shiloh County.
Frank Henry	Democratic county judge for Shiloh County and Judge Bass's election opponent.
Tom Blaine	A Democratic member of county government and a political confederate of Judge Henry.

The Schools

Major Players:

Roy Martin	The first superintendent of the Shiloh County schools.
Bill Wheeler	The second superintendent of the Shiloh County schools and advocate of change, and the leader responsible for securing Shiloh County's Experimental Schools project.

Sam Collins	The third superintendent of the Shiloh County schools.

Supporting Players:

Ms. Flowers	A Washington, D.C., employee of the Experimental Schools program, responsible for monitoring Shiloh County's Experimental Schools project.
Mr. Season	Ms. Flowers's replacement. He had the same duties.
Drs. Williams and Jones	University consultants to Shiloh's ES project with expertise in diagnostic instruction and proposal writing.
Drs. Frankel and Ribbon	Consultants to Shiloh's ES project with expertise in behavior modification.
Drs. Morris and Chalmers	Consultants to Shiloh's ES project with expertise in elementary mathematics.
Drs. Millsap and Lampkin	Consultants to Shiloh's ES project with expertise in Learning Activity Packets.
Mr. Beam	A psychologist who offered counseling to teachers, students, and parents during one phase of Shiloh's ES project.
Ms. Reid	A consultant to Shiloh's ES project with special expertise in reading.

CHRONOLOGY OF EVENTS

DATE	COMMUNITY EVENTS			COUNTY EVENTS	SCHOOL EVENTS
	South Shiloh	Cuba Landing	Clarksville		
1800	Settlement begins	Settlement begins	Settlement begins	Settlement begins	
1829				County incorporated	
1850				Magisterial districts formed (unchanged until 1976)	
1890	Population apex	Population apex	Population apex	Population apex	
1893					Shiloh county has 46 schools
1914				Mr. Henderson elected to state legislature	
1927					Buck Snort School built with volunteer funds and labor
1939				County voted dry	
1940					Buck Snort High School consolidated with Clarksville High School
1948			Floodwall		
1955		Tile factory			
1960	End population decline	End population decline	End population decline	End population decline	
1963		$50 million bond issue			Severe crowding begins
1968				$150 million bond issue	Crowding worsens; in-lieu-of-taxes agreement made
1969					Property taxes increased; utilities use and franchise taxes imposed; industry sues; industry hires social research firm to survey schools
1970				Planning and zoning commission formed	School survey made public; contains 19 recommendations for educational change
1971					Statewide teacher strike; Superintendent Martin dies; Wheeler hired as superintendent; Wheeler accepts survey recommendations as a blueprint for change; state facilities survey requested; Wheeler recommends new consolidated high school and interim operation of Buck Snort elementary school

DATE	COMMUNITY EVENTS: South Shiloh	COMMUNITY EVENTS: Cuba Landing	COMMUNITY EVENTS: Clarksville	COUNTY EVENTS	SCHOOL EVENTS
March 1972					Experimental Schools program announcement of a competition for small rural schools; Wheeler applies on behalf of Shiloh's schools
May 1972					ES site selection team visits Shiloh
June 1972					Shiloh County chosen as ES site
August 1972					First two project coordinators replaced by coordinators "loyal" to Wheeler
November 1972					*Shiloh Crier* article proclaims, "Our Schools . . . They're On Their Way"
August 1973	Blaine and Henry talk to Wheeler about school for Buck Snort			Pre-election politics Payroll tax imposed	*Shiloh Crier* article on board of education petitioning state department of education for new school at Buck Snort
					Three-week workshop to introduce teachers to Wheeler's ES program
					Consultants to mathematics program tell teachers individualized instruction will not raise achievement test scores
September 1973					Beginning of ES program implementation
					Drs. Williams and Jones introduce diagnostic instruction to teachers
October 1973		Election campaigns	Election campaigns	Election campaigns	Diagnostic instruction workshop on educational taxonomy; teachers resist Dr. Jones
					Wheeler confronts high school teachers on lax janitorial standards; rebuffed; teachers complain to school board members
	Buck Snort delegation visits board of education				
November 1973		Robbins elected mayor	Harold elected mayor	Henry elected county judge	

CHRONOLOGY OF EVENTS (continued)

DATE	COMMUNITY EVENTS: South Shiloh	COMMUNITY EVENTS: Cuba Landing	COMMUNITY EVENTS: Clarksville	COUNTY EVENTS	SCHOOL EVENTS
December 1973				Ambulance service continued	Middle School's reading center draws consultant praise Teachers cannot discriminate between scope and sequence and curricula continua; Wheeler says, "I see no hope."
January 1974				Wheeler and Judge Henry in open conflict	
February 1974	Meeting held in Buck Snort School; Wheeler asks audience to have faith in him and board of education	Landing protests Wheeler's plans for cafeteria		Governor announces construction to begin on four-lane highway between Landing and Clarksville	Consultants discover teachers have not prepared learning activity packets; task group reorganization; anonymous telephone calls protest ES program
March 1974	Buck Snort delegation visits state department of education			Pine Wood Park purchased	Learning activity packet task group reorganization breaks down; teachers go to classrooms Beginning of split between Wheeler and chairman of board of education
April 1974		Landing delegation visits board of education to discuss cafeteria		Operation Helping Hand	Teacher delegation visits board of education to protest Wheeler's leadership Mathematics program dropped in middle school
May 1974	Wheeler agrees to renovate Buck Snort School			Band Boosters begin to oppose Wheeler	Board of education refuses to fire band director; grants him tenure
June 1974					Wheeler tells board of education he will not ask for a new contract; chairman of the board told by a teacher to consider Collins as next superintendent
August 1974					Teachers ignore Wheeler at workshop; Wheeler threatens Collins with reassignment; teachers and board member support Collins Reading and math achievement test scores down from 1973 levels Drs. Williams and Jones introducc blue book to teachers; assume agreement

DATE	COMMUNITY EVENTS			COUNTY EVENTS	SCHOOL EVENTS
	South Shiloh	Cuba Landing	Clarksville		
September 1974					High school accredited by Southern Association of Colleges and Schools; Reading system becomes supplemental to traditional teaching; Mr. Season says learning activity packets are miniature textbooks; Dr. Millsap agrees
October 1974				New ambulances	Teachers reject blue book, rebel against Dr. Jones and diagnostic instruction
					Students strike at high school
					Student delegation visits board of education to protest ES program
November 1974					Lead teacher group formed to act as change agents; teachers again reject Drs. Williams and Jones
December 1974				Shiloh applies to HUD for money to refurbish court house	School programs filmed by state educational television; teachers complain to board of education
					Dr. Frankel admits his program of behavior modification will not work in Shiloh's schools
January 1975					Board of education offers Wheeler a new contract; intense political activity in opposition to contract
					Wheeler resigns
February 1975					National Institute of Education review panel visits Shiloh schools
March 1975					Wheeler announces his acceptance of a position in another school district; Collins appointed as superintendent
August 1975					Collins delegates responsibility for ES program to project coordinators
May 1976					State facilities survey team visits Shiloh
August 1976	New elementary school			Court house decision; magisterial redistricting	State facilities survey recommendations made public; negotiations over school site begin

Part 1

Community and the Politics of Developmental Change in Shiloh County

1

The Sociocultural Context of Developmental Change

My effort to understand the process of developmental change in Shiloh County began with a consideration of the sociocultural context for its political decision making. Although the most salient frame of reference often varies from situation to situation, affiliation with family, neighborhood, church, community, or even Shiloh County itself is an important basis for most efforts to command political loyalties. Through the skillful manipulation of these "contextual variables" individuals and groups in Shiloh are aligned in various shifting coalitions to affect both discrete and ongoing political actions.

The basic frame of reference in Shiloh County is familialism, a sense of loyalty based upon the recognition of kinship. It begins with the nuclear family, is conferred upon the extended family, and is finally expanded to include what residents call "kin, kinfolk, or relatives."

A second frame of reference in Shiloh relates familialism to neighborhood. A 1940 county map delineating social boundaries identifies twenty-eight rural neighborhoods scattered throughout Shiloh. Nineteen of the neighborhoods bear family names. Of the remaining nine, six denote local features (e.g., Frog Lick, Lonesome Hollow) and three honorifics (e.g., West Point). A school map drawn in 1933 shows one-room rural schools named after the leading families in each of these neighborhoods.

A third frame of reference is organized religion. A 1970 census shows that 5,207 people, or 73.9 percent of Shiloh's residents at the time, claimed membership in one of the county's churches. While nationally organized religion holds sway over the entire county, residents usually identify themselves as members of a neighborhood church. The 1970 census shows twenty-five local churches in Shiloh (twelve Southern Baptist, eight United Methodist, three Catholic, one Cumberland Presbyterian, and one Pentecostal Holiness). The Southern Baptists constituted the majority faith with 3,314 members; the United Methodists were second with 1,033 adherents; the Catholics were third with 698; and the Cumberland Presbyterian and Pentecostal Holiness churches came in last with 31 and 26 members, respectively.

Community is the fourth frame of reference in Shiloh County. There are two levels of community in the county. At one level are the three locally recognized aggregations of rural neighborhoods: South Shiloh, Cuba Landing, and Clarksville. At another level, Shiloh itself is regarded as a community, an example of the southern county where, "The county itself was the unit of dispersal and assemblage."[1] When dealing with local affairs, an individual is a member of a familial unit, a neighborhood, a religion, or a community; when dealing with external agencies, an individual is a "Shiloh Countian."

FAMILIALISM

In Shiloh first loyalties are reserved for members of one's nuclear family, one's extended family, and one's other kin. The importance of this familial frame of reference is a consequence of the history of the county, which was first settled by groups of families around 1800. One group carried the traditions of the plantation South and colonized the alluvial floodplains along the river. These families used slave labor to clear and tend large tracts of land and developed a cash crop economy. Another set of families carried the traditions of the hill South and colonized the hills and coves south of the river to practice subsistence agriculture. Between 1800 and 1890 descendants of families in both traditions settled near ancestral homesteads and relied on one another for help in farming and such communal efforts as the establishment of churches and schools. From 1890 until 1960 Shiloh's economic and demographic fortunes declined. Residents of the county adapted by strengthening family ties. Land in both the alluvial floodplains and in Shiloh's hills and coves remained in the family. "Farms pass down from generation to generation – just like in the Bible," explained one woman. The importance of familial ties was emphasized by a man without local kinship affiliations. "Hell. I've been here twenty years and they still call me an outsider," he said.

A familial unit contains a large number of people. At one family reunion, 177 people, nearly all of whom were related to one man, his wife, and their married daughters and spouses, gathered on a farmstead in Shiloh's hill country. The day was spent sharing a dinner that had been three days in preparation, enjoying the music of a country and western band, and renewing social ties. While a large share of the conversation focused on family matters, discussions also concerned political events in Clarksville and Cuba Landing, the Shiloh County Fiscal Court, and the school system. The participants knew their subjects: they either served as elected officials or were employed by the organizations they discussed.

Such political discussions underline the importance of the family as a basis for political power in Shiloh County. Kinsmen help one another, and elected officials are representatives of one or more familial groups. When Fred Harold won the Clarksville mayoral race, a Methodist minister noted that Harold was a member of two familial units, one by birth and the other by marriage. "All he had to do was to get the families to vote for him," said the minister. But there was more to the election than that. Harold ran for office as the head of a slate of candidates, each with his own familial backing. The slate therefore represented a coalition of many familial groups.

Familial ties are also basic to the staffing of local institutions. During one school year eleven married couples were employed as either teachers or administrators in Shiloh's schools. One family was represented by two generations and another by three siblings. If school support personnel and familial relations through secondary affiliations are included in the count, the Shiloh County school system looks like a node in the county's kinship networks rather than an independent organization. As a county politician said of Shiloh, "We're like a big family."

Family loyalties help assure adequate staffing of the school system. Because Shiloh cannot pay competitive salaries, school superintendents have recruited local college graduates by emphasizing proximity to family as an offset of low pay. Younger teachers recall Roy Martin, the superintendent, calling upon them as they neared graduation; he appealed to their sense of familialism to persuade them to ignore the problem of substandard wages and return to Shiloh. Martin was successful: 50 percent of Shiloh's teachers were born and raised in the county. Many of the remaining 50 percent married within the county and thus became members of familial units.

The extent of familial ties within the schools has had some obvious consequences: interaction is personalized, older teachers have taught two or three generations of the same families, younger teachers are beginning to teach the children of their own high school classmates, and still younger teachers are teaching their own siblings. Asked about the problems such familiarity creates, high school students said that all current teachers should leave the system, and the administration should reach outside the county to hire "someone who doesn't know us."

Although some teachers have become residents of the community served by the school, others do not consider community residence wise. As one teacher explained, "Trouble starts in the schools and winds up in church," where considerable social pressure can be exerted on school personnel. It is best not to be present in church and subject to patron pressures beyond school boundaries. Thus, many of Shiloh's teachers commute: all of the teachers in the Buck Snort Elementary School live in Clarksville; 50 percent of the teachers in the Cuba Landing Elementary School commute; and 30 percent of the teachers in the Clarksville Elementary School do so.

Kinship also influences political decisions made within Shiloh's school system. One incident is enshrined in county folklore. An older teacher in Cuba Landing's elementary school took her classes outside the building during the heat of spring and fall. Her principal, who was without local family ties, objected to her practice and posted notices forbidding it. When the teacher ignored the notices a dispute ensued, which was settled in the teacher's favor. She had been a classmate of a member of the board of education for twelve years, and her cousin was that member's wife. "We take care of our own," kinsmen say. The principal's contract was not renewed.

Another illustration of the political influence of kinship in the school system concerns the selection of candidates for the superintendency. One resident was opposed to the candidate who seemed to be the school board's likely choice and demanded that another applicant be considered. Local observers noted the family ties between the advocate and applicant and concluded that kinship was the advocate's motive. But since the board's choice was also a native with extensive family ties who had lived in all three major communities in Shiloh and served in the schools for over twenty years, his constituency was more powerful. The chairman of the board "knows what he's doing," said a local politician.

Indeed, the chairman did. During the selection process, familial delegations visited school board members and other elected officials to advocate the appointment of this or that candidate. One teacher recalled such a visit. The school board member gathered the delegation in his kitchen, shut the door, and guaranteed that nothing that was said would leave the room. "Let's talk family," he said, and they did. The discussion ended with agreement on the chairman's choice.

NEIGHBORHOODS

Kinship combines with locale to produce Shiloh's neighborhoods. In this respect Shiloh reflects the residential pattern noted by numerous observers of the rural South.[2] Shiloh's neighborhoods also exemplify the rural tradition of "neighboring." Neighboring is informal interaction among people living in close proximity and helping one another through life's vicissitudes. A good neighbor gives help freely, without being asked.

Shiloh's rural neighborhoods were most highly developed in the late 1800s, when neighboring helped build schools and churches, maintain graveyards, clear virgin land, and harvest crops. But from 1890 until 1960 people left Shiloh, sapping the strength of neighborhoods. Despite the loss of population, the tradition of neighboring has persisted, and examples of it abound. In Barlow Hollow, a rural neighborhood near Phillips, a man suffered severe illness one fall and was not able to harvest his tobacco. His wife said the crop was saved by "fine neighbors." Neighboring provides protection as well as assistance to those in need of it. As a folk saying has it, if the people of a neighborhood do not know you, "You don't belong there."

The practice of neighboring united the entire county one spring when a tornado struck a nearby community, killing thirty-two people and almost destroying the town. Within a week, Shiloh residents rallied to augment relief efforts: the Shiloh County Fiscal Court lent county equipment and personnel to a day-long volunteer effort dubbed "Operation Helping Hand"; the Board of Education provided two school buses to transport volunteers; the *Shiloh Crier* and Radio Station Clarksville publicized the effort; the chamber of commerce donated $1,000; and the churches acted as collection points for food and clothing. Operation Helping Hand recruited a team of seventy volunteers, along with a mile-long cavalcade of county, school, industrial, and privately owned equipment. The trip took two hours.

At the site of the disaster three groups of male workers were formed from among the volunteers. Two groups helped farmers clean their fields; the third stayed in town to raze a damaged church. (This pleased Catholics and Methodists, since they rarely had the chance to be good neighbors and tear down a Baptist church at the same time!)

Neighboring produces strong political action groups united by common local concerns. A group of neighbors from Buck Snort complained to the board of education that the disciplinary procedures in the Buck Snort Elementary School were too severe; discipline was subsequently relaxed, despite protests by teachers. When a group of neighbors from Tick Ridge complained about a school bus driver's reckless driving and "overbearing attitude," the driver was forced to resign. A group of neighbors from both the Cuba Landing and Clarksville neighborhoods convinced the Shiloh County Planning and Zoning Commission to reject two sets of coal-loading facilities planned for their neighborhoods; the tipples were located in adjacent counties. Finally, groups of neighbors from both Buck Snort and Phillips lobbied the fiscal court for roads and improved ambulance services; the fiscal court granted their requests.

RELIGION

Organized religion is an integral part of the culture of the American South,[3] and Shiloh County, where over 70 percent of the residents attend church services regularly, is no exception. Asked why ordained ministers are exempted from the county's payroll tax, a Shiloh politician explained, "We take our ministers seriously."

Again reflecting the pattern that prevails throughout the South, organized religion in Shiloh County is characterized by local autonomy. Southern Baptist ministers are invited to serve local congregations; they can also be dismissed by their congregations. Therefore, ministers tend to tailor their messages to local audiences. As a

Baptist explained, "A visiting preacher can say anything," but a regular minister must serve his flock of families and neighbors.

The Southern Baptist model – local choice of ministers and control of their tenure – is emulated by other Protestant churches, even those in which assignment of ministers is externally determined. Although Methodist ministers are assigned to local congregations by church superiors, Elmora Matthews, the wife of a Methodist minister serving a rural church in Tennessee, has noted the congregation's resentment of "higher church representatives such as the Methodist District Superintendent. They resent 'orders that are handed down to the small church.' "[4] What is true of a Tennessee Ridge community is also true of Shiloh. If external orders result in the assignment of a minister who does not meet with local approval, the minister is rejected. One Clarksville Methodist minister who did not meet with local approval discovered that his congregation was attending services in Cuba Landing and lobbying his church superiors for a replacement. The congregation got what it wanted.

The county's traditions of familial ties and strong neighborhoods also affect religious practice. An individual is not merely a Southern Baptist, Methodist, or Catholic, he is a member of a local congregation composed of kin and neighbors, as evidenced by a local celebration of the nation's bicentennial. The Clarksville Baptist minister organized a one-day revival that he called "Faith Day." Members of all the local churches were invited to attend, and a guest revivalist was the featured speaker. However, before the event took place, the minister suffered a heart attack. His replacement, a Cuba Landing Methodist minister, followed the agenda but imported a Methodist revivalist. The guest speaker delivered a long, loud, fervent, and fundamental sermon to the faithful, who were seated in the bleachers of the Shiloh County fairgrounds. But the crowd was smaller than expected. An observer gave two reasons for poor attendance: the Methodists were a minority faith and could not attract as large a crowd as the Baptists, and a Cuba Landing minister could not attract a crowd in Clarksville because he had no constituency there.

Shiloh's local churches exert influence on the county's informal patterns of social control. For example, one member of a Southern Baptist congregation in South Shiloh had a habit of cursing and thus behaving in an unchristian manner. Since repeated warnings did not alter his behavior, he was "churched," or excluded from the congregation by means of social isolation. The man was shunned by his neighbors, all of whom were members of the congregation. Similarly, a teacher who compared the leadership styles of Christ and Hitler in her classes was warned by kinsmen that making the comparison could lead to her exclusion from the church.

The churches also influence political events in the county. An 1853 edition of Shiloh's newspaper carried competing advertisements by sellers of alcohol and the Sons of Temperance. In 1939 the ideological descendants of the Sons of Temperance, led by Protestant clergymen, managed to vote Shiloh a dry county. When industrialization brought new residents, there was speculation that they would support a petition to place Shiloh's temperance policy on the ballot. However, the Protestant churches took public stands against the petition, and it gained little support. As one resident explained, the issue would have passed if put on the ballot, but the churches vowed to publish the petition in the *Shiloh Crier.* This would have subjected petition signers to considerable social pressure, and new residents were thus coerced into dropping the initiative.

Religious affiliation is a potent political force in another way: members of a particular faith tend to support comembers in the voting booths. Shiloh's county judge explained, "Hell. There's politics in everything, even where you go to church." But the religious support for political candidates goes even farther than the judge's analysis. One Republican candidate for the county judge's position lost the support of his fellow Baptists because he allowed his children to attend a fund-raising picnic sponsored by the Catholic Church. After his defeat at the polls, the candidate curbed his children's ecumenical activities and won the county judge's position in the next election.

The relationship between religion and politics is not one way; political events also affect particular congregations. When Fred Harold and George Chesney headed rival slates of candidates for Clarksville's city council, the election campaign split the congregation of the local Baptist Church. Both men had a following in the congregation: Harold's candidates were all members of that church, and Chesney was the choirmaster. After the election was over, a politician of a different faith analyzed the situation. "It'll take a revival to put that church back together," he said, and he remarked that having two candidates for the same office from the same congregation was rare. "They [generally] won't run against each other," a fact that makes campaigning difficult because of the potential bloc of votes based on religious affiliation.

One event pitted a church against a new subdivision inhabited by newcomers to the county. The symbolic contest marked a decline in the influence of organized religion. Despite zoning ordinances restricting building within the subdivision to single-family dwellings, a church bought a lot and prepared to build a neighborhood service center. Residents invoked ordinances to halt construction, and for the first time the efforts of a neighborhood church were thwarted in Shiloh. As one minister observed, the subdivision "doesn't belong to anything," because it is not dominated by kinship, neighborhood or religious ties.

COMMUNITY IN SHILOH

Just as familialism, territory, and local churches combine to produce neighborhoods, so do neighborhoods combine to form the major internal subdivisions within Shiloh that residents call "communities." There are three such communities in the county: South Shiloh, Cuba Landing, and Clarksville. Because Shiloh's topography ranges from alluvial floodplains to hills and coves, the county was settled by families that established two different patterns of residence. The frontier or open country neighborhood is found throughout the hill South, from the Appalachians to the Ozarks.[5] The open country neighborhood is a sociocultural unit with well-defined territorial boundaries and a fluid authority structure. It includes small subsistence farms and crossroad hamlets and is bound together by social ties forged in kinship, neighboring, and religious affiliation. This pattern of residence was extended westward after the Revolutionary War, when family groups of Scotch-Irish ancestry left the hills of Virginia and the Carolinas to colonize a new frontier, which was to become South Shiloh. The mountain folk settled in the hills and coves south of the river because the hilly land could be cleared by family, kin, and neighbors, and a single family could practice subsistence agriculture. Sons settled near paternal homesteads, thus creating closely knit neighborhoods that form this type of community.

The second pattern of residence was established by families from Virginia's tidewater region, who took advantage of Revolutionary War land grants to settle in virgin floodplain. Pioneers colonized the flat lands and deep alluvial soils along the river in what would become North Shiloh and formed plantation communities.[6] By 1840 North Shiloh embraced the Cuba Landing and Clarksville communities, areas that contained several large plantations, each tended by 90 to 100 slaves; had a caste-like social structure; and depended upon a cash crop economy.

That the variation in Shiloh's settlement patterns reflects cultural patterns is indicated in a number of ways. Plantations and hill farms contrasted with one another from the beginning. Plantations were large – up to 5,000 acres; hill farms were small – about 100 acres. Slavery was accepted in plantation country; hill people were ambivalent about it. A folktale about a hill farmer who owned several slaves during the Civil War illustrates this difference. His kin advised him to sell his slaves before the federal government required emancipation. He said he had never bought or sold men and would not sell in order to avoid financial loss, but neither did he free his slaves. The contrast in cultural patterns is also reflected in census data. The 1870 census recorded 898 Negro residents in Shiloh; 882 lived along the river and only 16 lived in the hills.

Cultural differences between communities have had political consequences. National partisan organizations have been represented in Shiloh since the founding of the Republican Party, but party membership and cultural boundaries were nearly isomorphic. Plantation country is traditionally Democratic, a legacy of that party's Civil War stand. In the hills the Republican Party was dominant. One folktale says the elections in Phillips, a hamlet in southeastern Shiloh, were unanimously Republican. Should a stray Democratic ballot be cast, "They'd hunt all winter 'til they found him" and then drive the deviant from the community by means of gossip and social avoidance. Shiloh residents say that cultural-political isomorphism is less pronounced now than it used to be, but fieldwork has indicated that it is still present.

Between 1890 and 1960 emigration destroyed the caste structure of the plantation communities in North Shiloh. Whereas the 1870 census records 898 Negro residents in the county, the 1970 census records 140 nonwhite (i.e., Negro) residents – all of whom lived along the river. And just as the lower caste emigrated, so did the upper caste. The same pattern of emigration affected Shiloh's open country neighborhoods (South Shiloh). What had once been strong, vibrant neighborhoods lost the majority of their residents. But because the population loss was spread fairly evenly between the two parts of the county, Shiloh's internal politics remained volatile.

Shiloh's major territorial components – South Shiloh, Cuba Landing, and Clarksville – are evenly matched political groups. These communities have their own agendas and practice the politics of developmental change to achieve community goals.

South Shiloh

There was no South Shiloh per se throughout most of the county's history. The hilly land south of the river was subdivided into many open country neighborhoods, each comprised of about four square miles, a church, a one-room school, and a small country store. In time, two hamlets, Buck Snort in the west and Minorsville in the east, became trading centers south of the delta, and the neighborhoods clustered around the hamlets were known as the Buck Snort and Minorsville communities. The dominance of the hamlets was solidified when each became the center of a separate census district and the polling place for electing a district magistrate (representing the third district in Buck Snort and the fourth district in Minorsville) to Shiloh County's fiscal court.

Then came population decline. Between 1890 and 1960 all of Shiloh lost people, but the Minorsville community was particularly hard hit. According to the Fifteenth Census of the United States, Minorsville lost 44 percent of its people between 1910 and 1930, Buck Snort and Clarksville lost 26 percent, and Cuba Landing lost only 16 percent.

Topography and farming practices explain the uneven emigration. Cuba Landing is in an alluvial floodplain, where erosion is minimal. Minorsville is in the hills, and Minorsville farmers plowed straight up and down their sloping lands. Thin topsoils eroded with each rainfall. When a plot lost its fertility, a hill farmer would sponsor a "log rolling." Kin and neighbors would congregate, the men to help clear a new five- or ten-acre plot, and the women to help prepare a communal meal. This worked until virgin land was exhausted at about the turn of the century.

Terrain in the Clarksville and Buck Snort communities contrasted with that of both Cuba Landing and Minorsville. The Clarksville area is a mixture of floodplain and hill country. Erosion did not affect this community's delta farmers, but it did wear away the soils of the hill farmers, who left to seek a living elsewhere. The terrain in the Buck Snort area is less rugged than the hills around Minorsville. Buck Snort's farmers therefore suffered less from erosion, and fewer of them left the community.

The prominence of Shiloh's open country neighborhoods also diminished as all-weather roads made consolidation of services practical, and various agencies eliminated local service centers. In 1902 there were nineteen rural post offices in Shiloh. The post offices disappeared with the advent of rural free delivery; by 1970 the county had only three: one each for Buck Snort, Cuba Landing, and Clarksville; the Minorsville Post Office was eliminated. The same type of change affected the school system. In 1893 there were forty-six rural schools; in 1970 there were four – again, Minorsville lost a service center. Minorsville became a ghost hamlet, hosting communal life only during Sunday church services, weddings, and burials.

The net result of emigration and service consolidation was the development of a belief system. The first item in this belief system was the existence of three communities in the county: South Shiloh, Cuba Landing, and Clarksville. Figure 1, which compares local conceptions of Shiloh's community boundaries circa 1900 with those of 1970, shows both the stability of community boundaries in the delta and the consolidation of Shiloh's open country neighborhoods south of the river.

Another item in the belief system was more localized. Whereas all of Shiloh normally subscribed to the three-community idea, South Shiloh was peculiar in that its residents refused to recognize community decline as a natural consequence of soil exhaustion. Instead, South Shiloh blamed its decline on decisions "they" visited upon the land: Minorsville had not become a ghost hamlet because the soil would no longer support the people; it had died because "they" took away the school and the post office and thereby forced people to leave.

South Shiloh's political stance is based on the belief that "they" have always treated South Shiloh unfairly, even to the point of calling South Shiloh "the back end of the county." To South Shiloh's residents, the contrast between the surfaced roads in the Clarksville-Cuba Landing communities and the graveled country roads in the south, which turn to deep mud with fall and spring weather, symbolizes this inequity. "We've always been here, but they don't pay any attention to us," said one woman. "When I pay my taxes, they don't knock anything off because I live in the southern part of the county," said another man.

Figure 1
Shiloh's Territorial Components

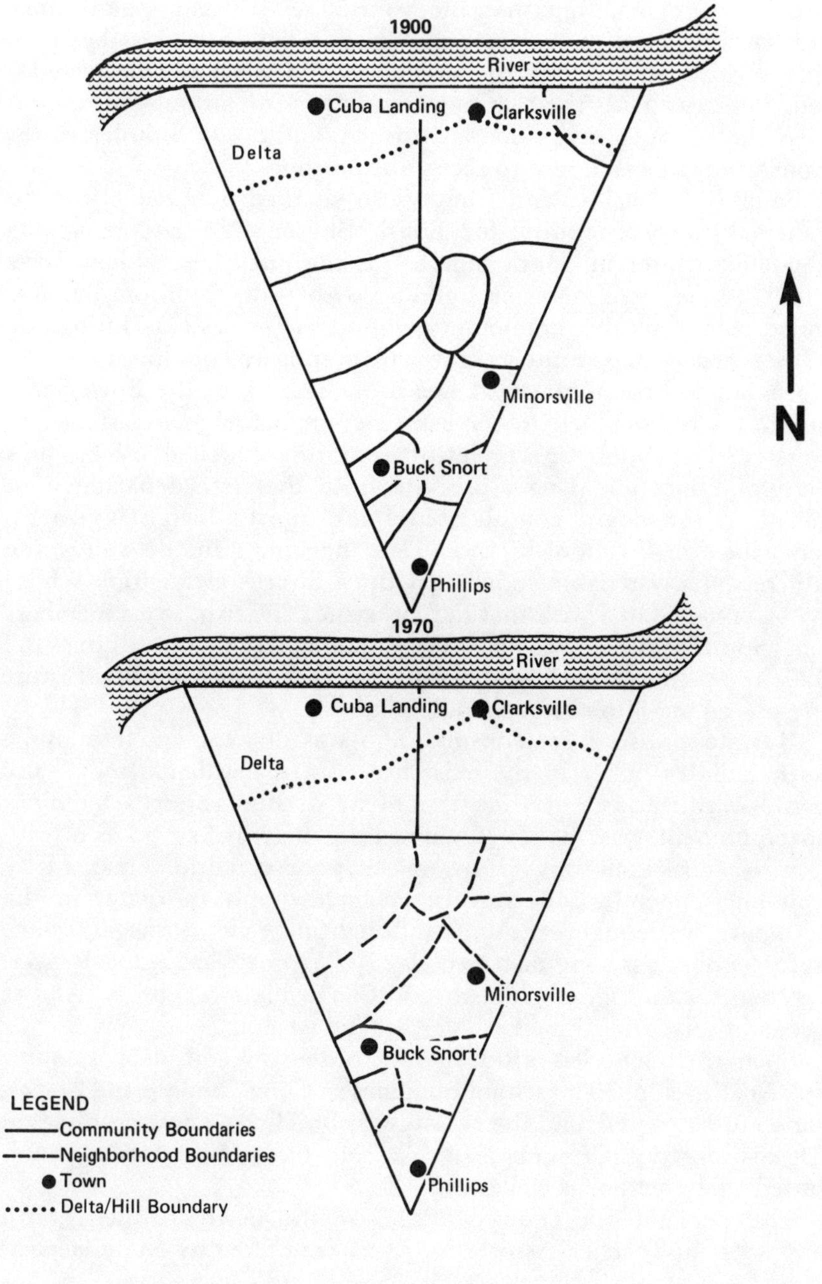

The condition of South Shiloh's roads led the magistrates from the third and fourth districts to team up in dealing with Shiloh's fiscal court, demanding that the court's service and maintenance funds be divided equally among all magisterial districts rather than being divided on the basis of population. Since a new county judge needed alliance with the two magistrates to form a three-vote majority in the court, a coalition was formed, and South Shiloh's roads, among other things, began to receive attention.

Belief in a malevolent "they" also sparked political efforts to attain educational equity for South Shiloh. The last remaining attendance center in South Shiloh was the Buck Snort Elementary School. A large wood frame building with four classrooms, it was funded and built by community volunteers in 1927. During the 1930s a group of volunteers traveled to another community to salvage a railroad roundhouse. It was brought back to the Buck Snort school and reassembled to serve as a combination gymnasium and cafeteria. But Buck Snort's effort was not matched by Shiloh's board of education. Under pressure from the state department of education, the board consolidated Buck Snort's high school with Clarksville's high school in the 1940s. Beginning in the 1960s, the state repeatedly recommended that Buck Snort's elementary school also be consolidated with that in Clarksville. The two board members from South Shiloh resisted the recommendation, but during the 1970s the sixth, seventh, and eighth grade students from Buck Snort were placed in Shiloh's new middle school.

If state pressure for consolidation was not enough to support South Shiloh's belief in the existence of a malevolent "they," the board of education's routine treatment of Buck Snort's buildings and equipment was. By 1970 the school that had stood as a testimony to local voluntary effort was in poor condition, marked by crumbling concrete foundations, stagnant pools of water in the basement, inadequate heating and lighting, and a sagging roof. As for equipment, one man explained, "We got what was left over. If a table wasn't good enough for Clarksville, we got it. And if they didn't have anything left over, we did without."

Such treatment led South Shiloh to demand educational equity with North Shiloh. The school buildings in Cuba Landing and Clarksville were renovated, and the county was building a new consolidated high school, football stadium, track, and bus garage. South Shiloh wanted a new school as well.

The demand for equity, voiced by the newly formed South Shiloh Parent-Teacher Association, was countered by State Department of Education officials, who used evidence of demographic trends as justification for denial. Bill Wheeler, Shiloh County's superintendent of schools, said that the state stand was backed by law; he and the local board had to comply. Under the leadership of Tom Blaine, an elected county politician from South Shiloh, the South Shiloh Parent-Teacher Association continued to press for a new school. The result was a struggle for control of Shiloh's school system.

The residents of Buck Snort also successfully forestalled the closure of their post office despite the fact that the Buck Snort hamlet and surrounding area were served by several different rural free delivery mail routes. The post office was very important to the residents of Buck Snort. As a community leader said, "A post office and a school are the heart of a community. Lose them and the community dies." Buck Snort residents, cognizant of the death of Minorsville and a host of other open country neighborhoods, were determined to save their community. The people were willing to enter into coalitions and play the politics of developmental change, if those politics were congruent with the politics of survival.

Cuba Landing

Cuba Landing is a river settlement where "uptown and downtown" mean "upriver and downriver." The community evolved as prominent families from tidewater Virginia colonized the delta land that would sustain the economic institutions of their civilization. By the 1830s, when Shiloh County was formed as a political subdivision, the Cuba Landing area contained plantations tended by slave labor, and the settlement came into being as a corporate entity.

The Landing's development was uneven. The nineteenth century treated it well: population increased and the river settlement prospered. Then the Landing went into decline, starting around 1890, when the river developed an appetite for the land upon which the town stood and, piece by piece, the Landing slid away. The community continued to decline as surfaced roads gave Landing area residents all-weather access to nearby urban areas. By the middle of the twentieth century the Landing was seen as a "sleepy little river town" that was slowly dying. This process was exacerbated by the emigration of prominent Landing residents seeking opportunity elsewhere.

In an effort to bolster the local economy, men from some prominent Landing families persuaded a brick company to set up a tile plant near town. While the plant provided jobs and a financial basis for improving city services, the factory was not large enough to stem the Landing's decline. Landing residents decided to obtain more help for their community by altering some of the laws governing systemic linkages between the Landing and the rest of the nation. Men from leading Landing families joined with representatives from other small towns and lobbied the state legislature for the right to issue municipal industrial bonds. The lobbying effort was successful, and the Cuba Landing City Council issued $50 million worth of bonds to construct a metal-processing plant near town. As a result, the Landing began to grow once again.

The social impact of growth can be measured in a variety of ways. The 1960 population was 610; in 1970 it was 1,595. The 1960 settlement pattern included a few grand old houses and a good many less-than-grand houses in the lower floodplains near the river. All were graced with roofed porches and porch swings, and most houses had yards with large shade trees. By 1970 air-conditioned, brick, ranch-style and split-level houses were clustered on low ridges in the Landing and on higher ground in adjacent areas.

Population growth had political impacts. The Landing's politics are played out in the city council by men who have consolidated communal frames of reference into stable political bases. Kinship is less a factor now than in the past because of the Landing's new residents. In an election for all six city council positions, John Horn's slate of candidates (promising "Better Government for Cuba Landing") defeated the "Citizens' Ticket," which was led by Bob Robbins, the incumbent mayor. The defeat was unprecedented in the Landing's familial politics, because the mayor's slate was composed of long-time residents with extensive kin networks, while Horn's candidates were relative newcomers to the Landing. A local explanation for the defeat was that new residents were not part of the Landing's kin networks. The new residents knew John Horn as a successful builder/realtor and the members of his ticket as businessmen supplying essential services.

The same explanation applies to neighboring. The candidates on the mayor's ticket had spent time and effort being good neighbors to the Landing's old residents, but had not expended the same effort on newcomers. On the other hand, the Better Government candidates were in frequent contact with the Landing's new residents because they sold essential services and thereby gained public visibility.

Before the election, Horn capitalized on the visibility of his ticket's candidates by mounting an outsider-versus-insider campaign. The first public exposure of this tactic came with newspaper coverage of the candidates' speaking performances before the Shiloh County Chamber of Commerce. The incumbent spoke first and defended his administration. "The Cuba Landing city government has done an excellent job," said the mayor. Under his leadership the city had attracted new residents, and plans were afoot for a new sewer project and water system, new recreation programs, and a new fire truck.

Horn rebutted Mayor Robbins. "I feel the city is at a standstill. The taxpayers of the Landing are being kept in the dark." He asserted that the only way to inform the taxpayers of city affairs was to commission a certified public accountant to audit city finances and then share the findings with the people. Horn promised to do so, saying that his ticket would "make the Landing the best place in the state to live, and a place which the people can be prouder of than [they are] today."

The next public exposure of Horn's outsider tactic was in the form of a political advertisement in the *Shiloh Crier* paid for by the Better Government ticket. The advertisement asked: "Do You Want A Better Government For Cuba Landing?" Horn's ticket would improve government by having a certified public accountant audit all city funds, by keeping all surplus money in the bank and collecting interest, by advertising for bids on city equipment, and by ending the promotion and entertainment fund.

The third public expression of Horn's outsider tactic was an attack on abuses of the promotion and entertainment fund. Due to church resistance to the sale of alcohol, all of Shiloh County had been dry since 1939. The entertainment and promotion fund was occasionally used to purchase alcohol in out-of-county settings. The Better Government ticket exploited the city council's defiance of local temperance in another paid political advertisement, this time against "the present City Council spending \$800 to \$900 annually at the Country Club for intoxicating drinks and steak dinners." The Better Government ticket promised an audit, bids on city purchases, continued efforts at securing a medical doctor for Cuba Landing, and improved services.

The voters elected all candidates on Horn's slate. This left Mayor Robbins, his appointed city utilities manager, and city employees as holdovers in a new regime and set the stage for a struggle for control of a local institution. At first, the Better Government group's voting majority held sway in public meetings. The first opportunity for the mayor to break this majority vote came with Horn's criticisms of city employees. The utilities maintenance foreman quit in protest, and the council found it impossible to replace him because no one with a thorough knowledge of city utilities would accept the job. The council requested that the mayor speak with the foreman, and Mayor Robbins did so.

The next city council meeting witnessed public admission that the Better Government group's voting majority was not all-powerful. Attending the meeting were the council members, Mayor Robbins, city employees, members of the press, and a host of Landing residents. To guarantee that no false rumors were spread, kin of the defeated Citizens' Ticket candidates tape recorded the event.

Mayor Robbins started the meeting by reporting that he had talked with the foreman and persuaded him to return to work. A councilman said the mayor had overstepped his mandate: the council had told Robbins to talk to the foreman, not ask him to return to work. The mayor's handling of the affair made it appear that the council was begging the foreman to return. Robbins asked for a reading of the minutes of the previous meeting, which a city employee provided; the minutes supported the mayor's actions.

The councilman would not concede. He told the foreman, "I think you're a good man. Good at your job. But I'm tired of this foolishness."

"It ain't foolishness," said the foreman.

The foreman's point was accepted by the full council, and he was formally reinstated. The new council had learned that a voting majority did not constitute absolute power in city government; there were contextual variables that had to be taken into account. Ed Dryden, the city's utilities manager, summed up the council's lesson: "You can work with those guys," he said.

Another chance to break Horn's coalition occurred during a discussion of city policy on gas main hookups. Horn asked the utilities foreman, "Who authorized you to stop hooking up meters?" "Nobody," said the foreman; but he explained federal regulations on hookups: "The federal people say you're accepting responsibility."

"Responsibility for what?" asked Horn.

"Gas and plumbing," said the foreman.

Dryden then read insurance regulations aloud. Horn said that nothing in the insurance codes prohibited hookups, and the city should continue to provide them. Dryden again cited federal regulations: "What're you going to do? Throw them out? Who's top dog? The federal government or the insurance company?"

The issue was settled when the council abandoned Horn and voted not to allow future gas hookups by city employees. The council's decision was deliberate: to support Horn's position would lead to the charge that the Better Government group was using city government to further the private fortunes of council members.

An opportunity to discredit Horn – and thus further weaken his coalition – came with the completion of the certified public accountant's audit of city finances, which showed that the Landing's government was adequately financed. The council refused to share this audit with the public, thus putting Horn in the position of promising voters information and then withholding it. The council did not make the audit public because news of the city's good financial condition might spark a taxpayer revolt. Collection of city property taxes was a sore point, and some property owners refused to pay them. The council proposed an innovation to handle past-due tax accounts: delinquent taxpayers would be sent a letter; if the letter produced no results, the names of the tardy payers would be published in the *Shiloh Crier.* A councilman asked, "They've already had letters, haven't they?"

"Yes," said Mayor Robbins.

"Then publish it," said the councilman.

The publication was to be written on city stationery and signed by David Roe, the city attorney, but Horn had an objection. "Let's back up. David, you're in business. I don't want to hurt one of your clients." An embarrassed client would transfer his legal business to another attorney.

"Hell. I'll sign. I wouldn't be in this business if I was afraid of hurting feelings," said Mayor Robbins, and the encounter ended with the mayor upholding the Landing's community interests in the face of special-interest opposition – with Horn as its spokesman.

Delinquent taxpayers were not happy about public notice of their unpaid accounts. One man said that the city deserved no tax money from him because it provided inadequate drainage for his property. Mayor Robbins had promised him that if he paid his taxes, the drainage problems would be solved. The man had paid, but drainage remained inadequate, so he quit paying city property taxes. "I know I owe my taxes. But I want some results after I pay [them]," said the delinquent.

"That's no reason for not paying your taxes," said a councilman, thus supporting the mayor's stand for community interests despite special interest lobbying.

The council also debated asking the fiscal court for additional police protection. Robbins suggested a familial alternative. "Do you want to approach the county or do you want to hire [a city employee's son-in-law]?" Horn wanted to approach the county. His suggestion prompted Robbins to say, "That's the reason we don't get any more done than we do. We're always hunting around to get someone to do something for us."

Horn demurred. "Let's see what we can get for free first." Kinship and community loyalty won out. The city employee's son-in-law was eventually hired, and the debate ended with another clear victory for Robbins.

Community loyalty also influenced local decisions when systemic linkages were imposed upon the council. One such situation occurred when Congress passed laws that granted floodplain communities the right to participate in a federally subsidized flood insurance program. Participation rules carried stipulations: no new construction could occur in flood-prone areas, and no federally guaranteed funds could be used to finance construction in either flood hazard areas or floodplain communities not enrolled in the insurance program. A Federal Insurance Administration Flood Hazard Boundary Map of the Landing showed all of the town, save for the ridge paralleling the river at the Landing's southern edge, to be in the floodplain. Robbins explained to the council consequences of this new systemic linkage between city government and federal agencies: "They've got a lock on us. [Without city participation] you won't even be able to borrow any money from a bank covered by federal insurance."

The council debated several possible courses of action in light of the floodplain legislation. Its first decision was to accept the provisions of the program that would benefit residents and to appeal stipulations that would limit the area available for further expansion. Robbins explained, "We want to write a letter to the government to say we want to become a part of the program so that residents can get flood insurance, but we don't agree with the map."

Disagreement over the flood boundaries drawn on the map resulted in a formal request for a restudy of floodplain boundaries. This prompted Horn to ask, "Is there any cost to the city?"

"No," said the mayor. The motion to write the letter passed without dissent.

The council later discovered that the public hearing that would accompany a restudy could jeopardize the city. Council members knew that the map indicated a greater area for expansion than was actually available. Should knowledge of the error be shared with the government through inadvertent disclosure during restudy hearings, the ridge that marked the Landing's southern boundary would be declared part of the floodplain, and the Landing would lose adjacent land for future growth. The council agreed that curtailing the Landing's further growth was not in the best interests of the community. The map and the constraints that it imposed were accepted because to challenge them would be to risk even greater community loss.

The sense of community that guided the council's decisions in the case of an imposed systemic linkage also affected its decisions to forge systemic linkages with other federal agencies. When the Department of Housing and Urban Development (HUD) announced that it had $8 million for rural governments in the state, the Cuba Landing City Council filed preapplication papers for inclusion in the program. A consulting engineer met with the council and outlined two different projects that HUD might finance. For $77,000 the council could pave Main Street and provide curbs, gutters, and sidewalks. A councilman objected that HUD would never put money into Main Street because it was a state-maintained road. The consulting engineer offered a solution. "If you all are going into this program, why don't you just take it back from the state? They're not doing anything for you anyway."

The engineer suggested a second project. For $217,000 the Landing could build a second elevated water tank. A councilman asked for clarification, and his question put into stark perspective the Landing's opportunistic strategy in forging systemic linkages.

"Which do you think we ought to shoot for?" he asked.

"Well, as far as need. . . "

"No. I mean as far as getting the money," said the councilman. The council accepted the engineer's recommendation to build the water tower. However, the application to HUD was subsequently denied.

The Shiloh County Fiscal Court wanted the Landing to join the City of Clarksville and the fiscal court in applying for a share of HUD's $8 million to renovate the county court house and part of Clarksville's central business district. The Landing's support of this application was important because HUD favored a policy of local government cooperation.

Cooperating with Clarksville went against the Landing's sense of community. The two towns had been rivals since the 1830s, and the tradition of competition was strong. The city manager tried to finesse the situation by saying there was a quid pro quo involved. "If the city council would support the fiscal court and the City of Clarksville, then next year they'd back us."

The ensuing debate again pitted Horn and Robbins in a leadership struggle. Horn called for a formal agreement: the Landing would support the joint application, provided that Clarksville's city council publicly promise to support the Landing's effort to gain a water tower next year. Robbins objected. "This is a gentleman's agreement. If our word is no good, neither are we."

"I'm not talking about our word. I'm talking about their word," argued Horn.

"I wouldn't rely on no promise from the City of Clarksville," interjected a city employee.

The city manager pointed out that the request for support came from Judge Henry, not from the City of Clarksville. Since Judge Henry had provided the Landing with more support than any other county judge, denying his request might jeopardize further fiscal court help for the Landing. Robbins and his supporters carried the debate. The joint application was filed because it was considered to be in the best interests of the Landing.

This debate and its outcome were characteristic of the relative political fortunes of Robbins and Horn. Robbins started as a clear loser. His Citizens' Ticket was swept from office by Horn's Better Government slate of candidates. But the mayor and his supporters slowly isolated and defeated Horn in the city council.

Landing residents ratified the mayor's tactics in the next city election. Mayor Robbins headed a city council ticket whose candidates were nearly all incumbents. Horn was reduced to running for mayor at the head of a ticket composed mainly of his kin. "He's trying to keep it all in the family," was a Landing assessment of Horn's slate of candidates. Horn lost the election; his kin group, which voted for him and his ticket out of familial loyalty, could not dominate the ballot box.

Clarksville

Clarksville is Shiloh's county seat and, as befits the center of county political debates, the town was sired by political intrigue. Shiloh's state charter fixed the county seat on a river farm donated by the Clark family. Clarksville thus hosts the Shiloh County Court House, the Shiloh County Board of Education, the home office of the Shiloh County Bank, and the branch offices of state and national bureaucracies.

Clarksville's preeminence in Shiloh has sparked resentment among the county's other communities. South Shiloh residents say that Clarksville has dominated the collection of tax revenues and has distributed public funds to Clarksville's benefit. Landing residents contend that Clarksville is a historical accident and hint at political skullduggery in the establishment of the county seat; they say that there is no community spirit in Clarksville.

Landing residents are partially correct about the last charge. While South Shiloh still reflects the open country neighborhood tradition and the Landing still has vestiges of the plantation South, Clarksville has no unitary history of its own. Containing both flat land and hill country, it is a river-town fusion of hill and plantation cultures. Located in the hollow along the river are the central business district, town hall, post office, county court house, board of education, and an older residential area; up on the hill, as it is called, are Clarksville's newer subdivisions. These disparate units seldom unite in a show of communal spirit.

Clarksville's population growth between 1960 and 1970 did not parallel the Landing's: the Landing gained 985 people during the decade while Clarksville grew from 882 to 1,262 residents – an increase of 380 people. Landing residents consider Clarksville's meager growth an accurate measure of the community's lack of dynamism, but the slow growth rate also left Clarksville's politics in the hands of men and women able to consolidate communal frames of reference and thus maintain stable political bases.

When the town's mayor retired in 1973, his council sought re-election en masse as the "Citizens' Ticket" and agreed that George Chesney, an incumbent councilman, should head the ticket as mayoral candidate. Chesney was the choir leader of the Clarksville Baptist Church; the rest of the ticket represented Clarksville's major families, neighborhoods, religions, and races.

The Citizens' Ticket was unopposed until the last day of filing for election, when it was challenged by the "Progressive Ticket," headed by Fred Harold, an assistant superintendent in Shiloh's school system, and representing the membership of the Clarksville Baptist Church. While the Citizens' Ticket had candidates representing all of Clarksville's neighborhoods, the candidates on the Progressive Ticket lived "up on the hill." The election thus pitted a slate of candidates that represented all of Clarksville's communal frames of reference against a ticket that represented only large family units, one religion, and one neighborhood.

There was only one public debate in which each candidate for mayor told the chamber of commerce about his platform. A coin was tossed to determine the order in which they would speak; Fred Harold lost and had to speak first, thus giving George Chesney the right of final rebuttal. Harold began with an appeal to familial loyalties. The Progressive Ticket was composed of "homegrown people who know the problems" and they wanted "a people-oriented government." The ticket would "lower water and sewer rates, blacktop all unpaved city streets, widen existing streets and install curbing and sidewalks, and attempt to consolidate the ambulance service, police and maintenance departments on a county basis." Harold promised to use his experience as a school administrator obtaining state and federal grants to secure the necessary money through revenue sharing. He concluded with an appeal to Clarksville's sense of community: "We will do what is humanly possible within the revenues available to make Clarksville a better city."

Chesney then took the lectern. He couched the Citizens' Ticket platform in ethical, religious terms: his city council would deliver "honest government represented with integrity and high Christian principles." This meant that he would "not make promises we cannot keep," like lowering local expenses by securing outside funds. Chesney also concluded his presentation with an appeal to Clarksville's sense of community: he and his associates were running for office because we "love our city and want to see it progress."

Clarksville voters retained all incumbent council members, but elected Harold as mayor by 288 to 260 votes, because in local terms he was only slightly less unpopular than Chesney. Harold thus became the nominal leader of a city council whose members were at least as representative, if not more so, of Clarksville's numerous contextual variables than he. A contest ensued to determine who controlled the city government.

The contest began with the budget. Mayor Harold assumed he had full control over the budget. Questioning some of his expenditures, the council passed a resolution requiring council approval for all city expenditures over $100. The *Shiloh Crier* began to carry stories about the shift in mayoral-council relations. The issue was publicly addressed in an article reporting that bids from two different paving companies varied greatly. A second article carried the city clerk's explanation that Harold "had put the wrong numbers on bid specifications." A later edition of the paper carried a letter from the mayor denying this public allegation of his incompetence: "The information was either incorrectly reported by the city clerk or misconstrued by the *Crier* reporter."

Without first consulting with Harold, the Clarksville City Council called a special meeting to delve into the matter. The *Shiloh Crier* was notified and represented at the meeting. An account of the special meeting was headlined "Tempers Bubble in Mix-up." Harold said his correspondence with both paving companies showed that neither had received the correct information and that mailing "is handled by the city clerk." But the city clerk insisted that the correspondence had been mailed out.

Harold sought to redirect the issue. "I'm not going to fight the war of who did or didn't, and I'm not going to be out over the fire about it. I've tried to legitimately do the best I can with the job I have. If I made a mistake, I apologize." But apologies were not enough; the city clerk proposed seven new operating procedures for council approval.

1. New locks should be installed on the city clerk's office and the office should be open during regular business hours only.
2. The city clerk should have the only key to the clerk's office.
3. The city clerk should be the sole person authorized to pick up mail at the Clarksville Post Office.
4. Copies of all correspondence written and received by the mayor should be filed in the clerk's office for future reference.

5. The city clerk should make records available only during regular business hours, and no records should be allowed to leave the clerk's office.
6. All money should be deposited in the bank by the city clerk.
7. All city documents and contracts should be the responsibility of the city clerk.

The mayor understood the purpose of these proposals. "It's pretty damn bad when the city clerk runs the city," he said.

The city council acted on none of the proposals, nor was it deemed necessary to appoint a new city clerk, because the council's lack of action served as a public announcement that political power was vested in the council. Thereafter the new mayor was simply one of seven popularly elected city officials rather than first among equals. This shift in power was reflected in the way meetings were conducted. Formerly, all elected members were seated at a table with the mayor at the head. Leadership came from his office, and meetings followed an agenda prepared by him beforehand. After the confrontation, council members and interested citizens brought up matters as they saw fit; the mayor's function was limited to answering questions, soliciting opinions, and agreeing to carry out the council's wishes.

The change in leadership and decision making left the council free to get on with city business: demands for change had to be weighed against a limited budget and certain consequences of raising taxes. As one Shiloh mayor said of city government, "The biggest problem is getting enough money to run it."

Clarksville's city government drew funds from a combination of local, state, and federal sources. These monies were sufficient to maintain existing services but not to expand them, and financial uncertainty stalked Clarksville's attempts at improvement. For example, an article in the *Shiloh Crier* said:

> In other matters, the council voted to postpone payment of $10,764 in paving jobs . . . . The councilmen agreed that it would be best, considering the city's present financial situation, if the payment would be halted until state reimbursement is received by the city.

Financial problems figured in other meetings. When the council considered raising city real estate tax rates, council members asked about the effect this would have on federal revenue sharing. "I'd say that we're going to lose on revenue sharing anyway," the mayor responded.

"Then I'm in favor of keeping the same rate," said a councilman. Without the justification of using local taxes to draw outside funds into city coffers, the council saw no reason to stir up voter antagonism by raising property taxes.

This meeting featured other city government attempts to use outside agencies in meeting Clarksville's needs. The council passed a resolution requesting that the fiscal court use a county bulldozer to widen a city street. When it was noted that the city hall needed a new paint job, Harold asked for an opinion. "Do you want to get city hall painted? Or get an estimate on it? Or what?" The council agreed to ask for a free estimate. Then the city clerk recalled an alternative solution. "The last time it was painted was by the woman's club," at no cost to the city. The problem of painting city hall was eventually solved by using Emergency Employment Act monies legislated by Congress and disbursed by county governments in rural areas. The fiscal court assigned one of its Emergency Employment Act personnel to paint Clarksville's city hall.

A more dramatic example of the Clarksville City Council's opportunism in forging systemic linkages with external agencies was the fiscal court's application for federal money to renovate the court house and part of Clarksville's central business district. As Judge Henry explained to the city council:

> This is a situation where the President has already approved the measure. Money is available. I'm coming here tonight with my hat in my hand. Shiloh County needs the support of the Clarksville City Council. In order to make this thing work, we need a joint proposal. The federal government and the state government want to see local governments work together. I think it's a wonderful opportunity for all of us. I'm here tonight to tell you we need you. We need you in the worst way.

"How much is this going to cost?" asked the city attorney.

"It won't cost the City of Clarksville anything. When it comes to cost, the fiscal court comes in," said Judge Henry.

"Would the fiscal court . . . hold us harmless?" asked the city attorney.

"Yes sir," said Judge Henry.

Mayor Harold stated his support of the application, noting that Clarksville stood to gain a great deal without venturing anything except a pledge to cooperate with the fiscal court.

"I can't see that we can do anything but get 100 percent behind it. It'll help us more than it'll help the county," said a councilman.

"I think it'll do more for Clarksville than any little thing we can do," said a second councilman.

The rest of the council agreed, and a motion was made, seconded, and passed to file a joint application for federal money. The Cuba Landing City Council also withdrew an application it had made to the same program in order to support the joint proposal. But federal funding of local projects presented another kind of problem. As Harold pointed out, the federal government talks one game and plays another. "They say they want local input, but they want federal control."

This observation led to the final curtain in the Clarksville City Council's leadership drama. Harold decided that he did not want to remain a nominal leader in a situation where the rule makers were allied against him, so he resigned in the middle of his term of office. The council appointed one of its members mayor and inducted George Chesney, its one-time leader, to fill the vacant councilman's seat. Once again, a local institution was in the hands of a group of people who could consolidate communal frames of reference into bases of political power.

Shiloh as a Community

Shiloh County exemplifies the southern county as a political unit whose subdivisions are within a day's horseback ride of the county seat. Though traditions may vary among the subdivisions, "the county itself [is] the unit of dispersal and assemblage."[15] Shiloh County emerges as a communal frame of reference when its residents meet individuals who live outside the county. To outsiders people always say that they are from Shiloh County rather than from a particular town or neighborhood.

The county served as a communal frame of reference when the fiscal court agreed to issue $150 million worth of municipal industrial bonds to finance construction of a metal-processing plant and a rod and cable mill because industrialization was "good for the county." The same frame of reference led the fiscal court to issue bonds to purchase pollution control equipment for the metal-processing plant; keeping the plant in operation and invoking standards of preferential hiring of locals were also considered "good for the county." When a local leader's position is in question, one factor weighed is his ability to attract outside funding for programs of developmental change. Finally, outsiders who advocate change see the county as a tightly knit social unit. As one advocate said, "The county's a closed system," implying that Shiloh acts as a unit in dealing with external agencies.

Two mechanisms that help to consolidate Shiloh's communities and their disparate value systems into a cohesive bloc in the face of external groups and pressures are Shiloh's communication networks and county-level political tactics.

Shiloh has informal and formal communication networks. Information flows through informal social channels created and fostered by kinship, neighboring, religious affiliation, and sense of community. Face-to-face and telephone conversations are used constantly to disseminate information. As one resident remarked, if one knew what went over the phone lines, one could "blackmail everyone in the county."

Shiloh's informal communication networks were important in forming county attitudes about Shiloh County's Experimental Schools program. Teachers resented parts of the program and spread rumors to discredit School Superintendent Bill Wheeler and his demands for program implementation. During this phase of teacher reaction to imposed educational change, Wheeler was said to be both intemperate and unchristian in his behavior. The intent of these rumors was to form a countywide constituency allied against Wheeler.

Formal communication is accomplished through the *Shiloh Crier* and Radio Station Clarksville. These two news organizations reach most of the households in the county. A 1974 survey showed that over 90 percent of the county's families read the newspaper and 85 percent listened to Radio Station Clarksville. Wide dissemination gives these two news organizations tremendous influence in shaping the issues of the day. Local decision makers have to take into account the influence of the news organizations, because a miscalculation can damage a public career – as Fred Harold discovered when he accused the *Crier's* reporter of an error in his story about the paving bid mix-up.

Most decision makers in Shiloh have an "understanding" with the news organizations that allows them to finesse what could be an adversarial relationship: reporters are allowed to know things if they do not report them. This understanding works most of the time. For example, the board of education had a meeting to decide whether to expel a student or allow him to graduate. The decision making started when Superintendent Wheeler said that, while the board usually went into closed session to discuss student problems, the press could stay if they promised not to report the discussion. The press agreed.

The student had come to high school under the influence of alcohol. The principal, Sam Collins, suspended the boy for three days and asked the board for guidance. One board member advised letting the boy graduate. Wheeler concurred but added, "If the boy comes back drunk again, we expel him." A teacher explained, "It was his birthday."

"Do you know him?" asked a board member.

"Yes."

"What do you think?"

"Let him graduate," said the teacher, and consensus was reached. No mention of the discussion appeared in the accounts given by either news organization.

This was not an isolated incident. When the fiscal court discussed reopening an abandoned road, a resident asked that it remain closed. "It's been a haven for your drugs. Marijuana Hill, that's what it is." The resident felt constrained about saying more. "I can't speak openly because I see a member of the press," she said. Judge Henry reassured her: "I think I've had an understanding with the news media. Any time we meet, the news media has been notified. Until we feel that we have been betrayed, they can attend." And so the press did attend and abided by a rule of "no notes and no disclosure" upon request.

The *Shiloh Crier* is not merely a conduit for disseminating political decisions; it also intervenes in the political arena in support of issues that the paper's management feels are in the county's best interests. One such intervention was on behalf of local beautification. The planning and zoning commission has the power to police land use in the Cuba Landing and Clarksville communities. The *Crier* charged that the commission was not meeting its duties; one site was an "eyesore." "We wonder if the zoning board could do something about the cleaning up of this particular place?"

The commission did so indirectly. The site was a few feet from a state-maintained road. According to state law, the state road commission had jurisdiction over all junkyards and dumps within 2,000 feet of a state highway. In the planning and zoning meeting that followed publication of the editorial, a commission member said, "Somebody should embarrass the foreman [and make the state enforce its regulations]."

"I'll take care of that," said the chairman.

Embarrassing the foreman began with the commission's public denial of responsibility. Members told reporters attending the meeting that junkyards were not a local problem but the state's concern. The commission gave reporters a letter that spelled this out: "An investigation of the sites . . . reveals that each of them falls within the jurisdiction of the Department of Highways." The letter became part of an article in a regional daily newspaper, and the publicity gained prompt attention from the state highway department.

Shiloh's teachers tried to use the *Crier* to publicize complaints about school conditions during the implementation of the Experimental Schools program. In the winter of 1974-75 a teacher arranged to have a nearby college offer a minicourse in journalism. The plan was to have college students supplement the staff of the *Crier* by writing feature articles on the Shiloh County schools. In early 1975 these students began interviewing school personnel about the new federal program.

The teachers were in an awkward position. They were unhappy about school conditions but reluctant to pit themselves publicly against Wheeler's authority as superintendent. An informal discussion in one teachers' lounge developed a strategy for handling the problem: "We had a meeting and everybody said they were going to lie. When you start to worry about telling the truth, something's wrong," said one participant.

The teachers' strategy did not work because the *Crier*'s senior staff members had heard too many tales of anguish from teachers. Reporters were sent back to interview the teachers a second time, especially those known to be unhappy about the federal project. After her second interview, one of these teachers claimed that the *Crier* already knew the answers and was simply using her to foment public discussion about the federal project.

The *Crier*'s senior staff members also used the telephone to interview teachers after school in an effort to gain more candid reports, and they arranged for interviews with Superintendent Wheeler. "There are two sides to every story," said a senior staff member. Referring to Wheeler, he remarked, "Some people think they pull the wool over our eyes – and we let them." But the newspaper's traditional arrangement with Shiloh's leaders intervened between interviews and articles. "We could have the best newspaper you ever saw. We could keep things in a turmoil all the time. But we don't in the interests of harmony."

One of the best examples of the *Crier*'s ability to intervene in political decision making occurred during the debate over the Shiloh County Court House. Although the fiscal court had filed a joint application with Cuba Landing and Clarksville for federal funding to restore the court house to its original condition, local opinion was divided. Most of the *Crier*'s staff believed that the court house should be saved. In one story on the debate the issue was presented in a seemingly objective way until a final interview:

> One outspoken citizen who does not believe that Shiloh County will receive federal funds believes it is "ridiculous" to renovate the existing Court House. He reminds citizens that "This is the twentieth century" where "we must grow and progress." He believes the present lot is of sufficient size – pointing out that other county court houses are built on lots comparable to Shiloh County's. "If we want to keep the court house, let's all get a horse and buggy," he concludes.

The story helped consolidate public opinion. One decision maker committed to saving the court house complimented the *Crier*'s staff on a fine story. He said the story had mobilized public opinion in favor of renovation. In particular, the final interview was a masterpiece because people reacted strongly against the speaker's attitude. This was no accident; the writer of the article said the final interview was solicited to unite support for saving the existing building.

Radio Station Clarksville followed a different news strategy from that pursued by the *Crier*. While the *Crier* served a local audience, the station sought a regional clientele. Shiloh was midway between two regional radio centers, neither of which dominated the local listening public. Local merchants were not served by an effective electronic advertising medium. Radio Station Clarksville set about altering this by marketing news. Reporters attended government meetings and local events throughout a four-county area, and accounts of these happenings were then aired as local news. At the same time, announcers told all communities in the listening area that they were part of the station's "Great Country." As Radio Station Clarksville gained hold of a regional audience, its reporters solicited advertisements from merchants throughout the listening area.

Regional coverage collided with Shiloh's sense of community. To overcome the potential handicap of the station's location in Clarksville, the station's management joined the Cuba Landing Lions' Club. While this helped integrate the station into the Landing community, it did not eliminate the problem of identification with Clarksville. Identification problems were magnified because the station personnel were not Shiloh natives and had little grasp of the county's traditions. This was clear when a Cuba Landing merchant was asked to sponsor a talk show featuring the high school basketball coach. The coach had been Clarksville's basketball coach before the consolidation of high schools, and Landing residents wanted him removed. The merchant feared that by sponsoring the program he would appear to be supporting the coach, and this would alienate Landing residents, who would trade elsewhere. Therefore, the merchant refused to sponsor the program.

Buck Snort presented another set of problems for Radio Station Clarksville. The village was not incorporated and had no formal government or politics to cover. Also, potential radio advertisers were leading the political effort to save Buck Snort's post office. They were using mailed advertisements to increase volume and thereby help justify the post office's continued existence. Furthermore, when the station publicized Shiloh's efforts in "Operation Helping Hand" the story failed to mention that South Shiloh's volunteers were the first to respond to the emergency. As a result, Radio Station Clarksville was given poor marks for coverage in South Shiloh.

Local decision makers and station personnel also had an "understanding" about news coverage which figured in reporting. The station was guaranteed access to news, but stories that would alienate decision makers were not to be aired without purpose. This agreement affected coverage of a student delegation complaining about conditions in the high school to the board of education. Since a student strike had preceded the delegation's formal complaints, news of the affair could not be kept from the public. Nevertheless, Superintendent Wheeler tried to minimize the flow of damaging information about his school system.

"You know this is going to be reported tomorrow," he told the delegation.

"What do you mean?" asked a student.

"On the radio."

"The more the better," said the student. The student delegation received only minor mention in newscasts.

County political tactics focus on consolidating Shiloh's communal frames of reference into stable political coalitions that can survive the balancing of unlimited demands against limited budgets. This balancing process pits communal frames of reference against one another in contests that have clear winners and losers. In Shiloh's terms, politics is the art of "doing" people and coalitions.

There are restrictions on "doing": losers in Shiloh's political trade-offs can use equity rules to disrupt coalitions. Decision makers therefore try to influence the flow of information to keep equity arguments from coming to the fore. Such considerations led to the informal agreement between the press and local politicians. The political process is further complicated because constituents demand that decision makers act as common men rather than members of an elite. "You get to thinking you're bigger than the people, they'll put the axe to you – real quick," said one successful county politician.

The most effective political coalition unites South Shiloh and Cuba Landing against Clarksville. During one primary campaign a candidate capitalized on the social ties forged in kinship, neighboring, and religious affiliation to win the support of party members in South Shiloh and then concentrated on Landing party members by reminding them that his opponents were from Clarksville. The primary was decided on the basis of kinship, neighboring, and religious affiliation in South Shiloh; the Landing's antipathy to Clarksville; and a split vote in Clarksville. These factors also overrode partisan political affiliations in the general elections and the candidate won easily.

Most general election campaigns follow the same tactics. While Democratic and Republican voter registrations are nearly equal (2,009 Democrats and 1,894 Republicans were registered in 1974), politicians say that people do not vote according to party lines. The best tactic, therefore, is to create solid coalitions based on nonpartisan considerations and then gain support in the remaining precincts by capitalizing on another candidate's social networks. Because of mutual need for support and the coalitions that mutual support creates, the Shiloh County Court House contains full-time, paid, elected officials from all of Shiloh's communities.

Coalition tactics were used in the 1973 race for county judge. The incumbent, Judge Ray Bass, was a native of Cuba Landing with Republican and Baptist affiliations. The Democrats chose Frank Henry as their standard bearer because he was also a native of Cuba

Landing. They knew that the Landing would vote according to residence rather than party membership and thus chose Henry to split the community vote. Both Bass and Henry campaigned hard: each attended public meetings in Clarksville, the Landing, and South Shiloh – usually in the company of politicians who dominated local social networks. There was one major difference in campaign style: Henry went from door to door and personally solicited support. His major argument was that, while Judge Bass's administration had attracted industry, industrialization had not led to developmental change. Henry promised that if elected he would seek out ways of sponsoring development. Judge Bass relied on his partisan supporters to do the political legwork, and his representatives spoke of retaining tested leadership, rather than misplacing trust in Henry, a callow youth of Catholic background.

Judge Bass's tactics failed; Henry won the general election. According to local observers, this happened because the two candidates split the community block vote. Furthermore, Henry's door-to-door campaign style characterized him as a common man concerned with Shiloh's lack of development. Even so, the vote was close, which local observers attributed to Henry's religion.

People with little knowledge of Shiloh see local events as indicating a decline in traditional antipathies. In a presentation to the chamber of commerce, a regional political figure said that the change of name – from the Clarksville Chamber of Commerce to the Shiloh County Chamber of Commerce – betokened a new county. He could remember when "Clarksville people would take the old Clarksville-Buck Snort road to market to keep from going through the Landing."

However, this new spirit of community ecumenism did not pervade the Landing. The new chamber name was mere word magic; the chamber did not represent "the western part of the county." This sentiment was given full voice by a Landing politician who said of the chamber, "All's they got is a few businessmen, a little industry, and the courthouse gang." History has given Shiloh communal frames of reference where first loyalties go to kin, neighborhood, religion, and community. In a county politician's analysis, "There's no such thing as a Shiloh Countian – there's fifteen varieties." To weld these varieties into a southern county that faces outside agencies and forces as a single unit takes considerable political skill which, as the rest of this volume demonstrates, is not beyond the capabilities of Shiloh's leaders.

Notes

1. Conrad M. Arensberg and Solon T. Kimball, *Culture and Community* (New York: Harcourt, Brace, and World, 1965), p. 106-107.
2. Elmora Mercer Matthews, *Neighbor and Kin: Life in a Tennessee Ridge Community* (Nashville, Tenn.: Parthenon Press, 1965), p. xxiii; John B. Stephenson, *Shiloh: A Mountain Community* (Lexington, Kentucky: University of Kentucky Press, 1968), pp. 2-3; Mandel Sherman and Thomas Henry, *Hollow Folk* (New York: Thomas Y. Crowell Company, 1933), p. 15; and C. Thompson Wacaster, "Jackson County: Local Norms, Federal Initiatives, and Administrator Performance" in *The Dynamics of Planned Educational Change: Case Studies and Analyses,* eds. Robert E. Herriott and Neal Gross (Berkeley, Calif.: McCutchan Publishing Corp., 1979), p. 115.
3. Arensberg and Kimball, *Culture and Community*, p. 107; Robert E. Herriott and Benjamin Hodgkins, *The Environment of Schooling: Formal Education as an Open Social System* (Englewood Cliffs, N.J.: Prentice-Hall, 1973), pp. 36-37; and Carol E. Hill, "Anthropological Studies in the American South: Review and Directions," *Current Anthropology* 18, no. 2 (1977): 312.
4. Matthews, *Neighbor and Kin,* p. 81.
5. Arensberg and Kimball, *Culture and Community,* pp. 108-111.
6. Marion Pearsall, "Cultures of the American South," *Anthropological Quarterly* 39, no. 2 (1966): 135-137.

2

The Politics of Developmental Change

Planned changes in the facilities and services offered by Shiloh County government – whether initiated locally or imposed by external agencies – are influenced by the communal frames of reference described in the preceding chapter. The narrative that follows supports the thesis that local political decisions are responsible for developmental change in Shiloh, even when the agent of change is federal policy or a federal agency. The fiscal court's programs of developmental change were structured around local political processes such that change was introduced in direct response to local needs, priorities, and strategies. The planning and zoning commission was the product of national policy, an imposed systemic linkage that played a role in the resolution of issues concerning land use. Shiloh's political processes intervened in the use of the commission as a systemic linkage to direct the course of this program of developmental change. Local political processes also determined the course of a program of developmental change designed to transform the schools in Shiloh County.

THE HISTORY OF SHILOH'S POLITICS OF DEVELOPMENT CHANGE

The county began as part of America's southern frontier, an agricultural society with two dominant value orientations: one conservative, characterized by submission to authority, conformity, and religious fundamentalism; the other pragmatically rational, favoring equality among Caucasians, Jacksonian democracy, and rugged individualism. The second orientation has become more pronounced as the South has "begun to break out of its ideological constraints"[1] to practice the politics of developmental change.

Just as the American South has exhibited a change in values, or what Lionberger called "important organizing themes in the behavior of individuals,"[2] so have Shiloh County's values changed.

There is no evidence that the county attempted to attract new industry in its first sixty years (1830-1890) of incorporation. Rather, the reverse is true. A cotton mill that sought to locate in Shiloh could not purchase a proper mill site because all suitable sites were the property of plantation families content with Shiloh's existing social order and opposed to industrialization and the "mechanic's society" it spawned.

Around 1890 the county's economic and demographic trends went into decline. During the next seventy years, from 1890 to 1960, the censuses show an average loss of 96 farms, 3,878 acres of farmland, and 555 people every ten years. Although the county had no natural resources that could be exploited in order to halt the decline, Shiloh's leaders were willing to use the expertise and resources of external agencies to improve local conditions.

The first such attempt at forging a systemic linkage was made in 1913. Jack Henderson, a resident of Cuba Landing's Frog Lick neighborhood, ran for state legislator. His platform was direct: the creek that cut through Frog Lick flooded every spring, ruining crops and farmers alike; the state should help the citizens of Frog Lick by providing the money necessary to dredge the creek. If elected, Henderson would introduce a bill in the state legislature to have the state pay for the dredging.

Henderson's platform won him the election: the voters of Shiloh supported his initiative to use an external agency to promote developmental change. But the state legislature was not willing to be used. Henderson's relief bill was first stopped in committee, then lost by the committee chairman. Henderson would have resubmitted his bill, had it not been the attorney general's opinion that it was illegal to do so. Henderson returned to Frog Lick empty-handed. Shiloh's voters did not reelect him, and the creek was finally dredged through local effort.

A second attempt to reverse Shiloh's decline was made in 1927. State printing and distribution facilities were used to produce a pamphlet that told of the county's industrial attractions: clay was being mined and shipped to manufacturers of roofing tile, sewer pipe, chimney tile, and kindred articles. The pamphlet described the county's shipping facilities, raw materials, and low power rates as attractive to both brick and tile manufacturers. But Shiloh's courting calls were ignored; manufacturers preferred to remain in more urban locales and import Shiloh's clay.

A 1931 economic inventory of Shiloh's geological resources offered an explanation of the county's declining fortunes. Significant portions of its resources had been depleted. Soils, which were developed from either alluvial or residual deposits, headed the list. The alluvial silts were replenished by flooding, but the residual soils, located in hilly terrain south of the river, had eroded because of poor farming practices. Subsistence farmers in the hills emigrated as the soil was exhausted.

Shiloh had also depleted most of its mineral resources. Coal had been important in Shiloh's history, but the industry went into decline in the latter part of the nineteenth century. Miners emigrated when the coal seams were exhausted. Although gas and oil had played a part in Shiloh's economic fortunes, the county's oil reserves were not great and had not resulted in a large influx of people. The inventory concluded: "There seem to be but slight opportunities for developing natural resources in Shiloh County except those of gas and oil and possibly clay." If the people of Shiloh were to improve the local quality of life, they would have to learn how to exploit other kinds of resources.

Shiloh began to learn how to do so in the 1940s and 1950s, as evidenced by Clarksville's dealings with the railroad. The railroad had discontinued depot service, and the city wanted to buy the depot for use as a city hall. The railroad offered to sell the building for $1,000. The city did not have the money, but a search of property records revealed that the depot was on city-owned land. The mayor made a counteroffer: the city would require $5,000 to remove the building from the city property – unless the railroad could accept a purchase price of $300. The railroad could, and the depot changed hands after the city borrowed $300 from the Clarksville Bank. Space was then rented to an express company for $30 per month, and the rental money paid the bank loan.

Shiloh's political ability to use external agencies to meet local needs was demonstrated even more clearly in Clarksville's response to conditions caused by the 1948 flood. A search of federal legislation revealed that federal flood control funds were available to any community that could demonstrate that prior flood control measures had adversely affected it. A floodwall across the river protected a neighboring community but constricted water flow, and a case was made that the displaced water drenched Clarksville. Congress accepted this argument after Clarksville raised $18,000 to match federal funding. The cost of the floodwall came to $750,000, which was $450,000 more than Clarksville's assessed valuation. Even so, the project was the smallest on the river – a fact that attests to Shiloh's ability to use outside resources for internal development.

During the 1950s Shiloh residents learned that the county possessed attractive industrial sites. New technology had made the mining of marginal coal deposits profitable, and local coal miners had been supplying coal to fuel brick factory kilns. The miners showed brick company officials samples of plastic fire clay derived from deposits juxtaposed with coal seams. Surveys demonstrated that the clay deposits justified opening a branch plant near Cuba Landing, and the plant began operations as a tile factory in 1955.

The Cuba Landing City Council capitalized on the plant's location by creating a municipally owned utility to service both city and plant. The utility service showed a profit, which was translated into improved services for Landing residents.

Initial industrialization was impressive but not spectacular. Although the plant provided jobs and public revenue, it did not stem the flow of emigration. Landing residents wanted more, and the knowledge that Shiloh had attractive industrial sites and that laws could be used to Shiloh's advantage led to a political lobbying effort. For years the state had allowed large cities the right to attract industry by issuing municipal industrial bonds. Influential Landing residents, men whose families had colonized Shiloh's delta land, joined forces with representatives from other small towns to persuade state legislators to extend the right to issue such bonds to small communities.

Cuba Landing's city council immediately entered into agreement with a large metal-processing firm. The Landing would issue $50 million worth of municipal industrial bonds, provided that the firm constructed a plant near town. The agreement was mutually satisfying. The Landing gave nothing more than its name to a paper bond issue that the firm would retire. Since the Landing was the nominal owner of the plant, the company was not obligated to pay local or state real estate taxes until the bonds were amortized and ownership had passed to the company. When site purchase costs exceeded the firm's budget, Landing residents raised $68,005 within two days. Although the money was subsequently returned to the donors by the company, one resident said, "It stands as an indication to the company of how we feel."

A metal-processing plant cannot function without cheap electrical power, so a regional utilities firm built an electricity-generating complex in Shiloh that supplied electricity at 3.5 mills per kilowatt hour, a rate lower than the national average of 4 mills per kilowatt hour.

Shiloh's industrialization had immediate consequences. When construction of the metal-processing plant began, a bridge was built across the river at Clarksville. This prompted two pulp and paper processors to locate an integrated facility near Clarksville, because the bridge gave greater access to both raw materials and market areas, and because the county had a "good attitude" toward industry. (The good attitude was necessary to mitigate the effect of pulp-processing odor on an area's residents.)

Shiloh's strategy for attracting industry received attention in two different groups of organizations. One group, the planning divisions of three metal-refining and -processing firms, wanted to locate near Shiloh. The Shiloh County Fiscal Court entered into agreement with these firms, issuing $150 million worth of municipal industrial bonds for the firms to locate in Shiloh. Once again, local effort was confined to bond issue; it was agreed that the firms would supply their own police and fire protection, road maintenance, water, and sewerage.

The second group of organizations to become interested in Shiloh's strategy for industrialization was the Congress of the United States and the Treasury Department. On February 15, 1967, Henry Reuss (D-Wis) introduced H.R.s 5484, 5485, 5519, and 5520 because local governments had been using Section 103(c) of the 1954 Internal Revenue Code in ways not intended by lawmakers:

> For over 15 years State and local governments have been abusing the privilege given by the Federal Government to issue tax-exempt bonds. Though intended as a Federal subsidy for much needed public facilities . . . tax-exempt bond issues have been floated with ever-growing frequency . . . to finance commercial and industrial facilities of private profit-making corporations.

> Giving birth to a municipal industrial development bond is painless. The town council need only agree to issue the town's bonds to pay for an industrial plant . . . The corporation then builds the plant in the town's name. The plant is paid for with the proceeds of the town's issue. The town then sells or leases the plant to the corporation for an amount sufficient to cover its principal, interest, and underwriting costs.
>
> Because the interest is tax free, these bonds sell at a lower interest rate than the bonds which the most credit-worthy corporations could issue. The savings in interest charges is the subsidy which the town uses to lure the corporation . . . On a $20 million, 20-year bond issue, a corporation might well save $5 million . . . And if the corporation buys the town's bonds, as many do, it receives tax-free income besides.
>
> We first became interested in municipal development financing when . . . Cutler-Hammer Corp., of Milwaukee, announced that it would pull up stakes and move a part of its operation to Bowling Green, KY. Bowling Green built Cutler-Hammer a new plant . . . . And Milwaukee lost 750 skilled labor jobs as a result . . . in the long run only the corporations will ultimately benefit . . . .[3]

Reuss noted that many organizations, ranging from the AFL-CIO to the Securities and Exchange Commission, opposed issuance of municipal industrial bonds as a strategy for industrialization, yet the Treasury Department had taken no action. Reuss urged it to do so.

The Treasury responded in written testimony before the House Ways and Means Committee. The gist of the testimony was that abuses had occurred in the issuance of municipal industrial bonds but that these abuses were legal under existing legislation. By setting an issuance policy that ran counter to legal mandate, the Treasury Department would be open to lawsuit. "Although the question is under study by the Treasury Department, clearly a legislative solution to this problem would avoid any future misunderstanding."[4]

Congress responded by amending Section 103(c) of the 1954 Internal Revenue Code to preserve tax-free status for bond issues under $1 million or for issues used to pay the cost of certain facilities, such as pollution control devices.

Legislative redefinition left the recipients of Shiloh's $150 million issuance in a bind. Planning and site acquisition had consumed several million dollars of company capital outlay, but the bonds that would finance construction had not been issued. These firms and others that stood to lose millions of dollars because of congressional action joined forces and worked out a protective grandfather clause with the staff of the Joint Ways and Means Committee. Shiloh's bond issue was saved, and industrialization continued in the county.

THE POLITICS OF DEVELOPMENTAL CHANGE IN THE SHILOH COUNTY FISCAL COURT

The Shiloh County Fiscal Court is the county's governing body. The court meets in the Shiloh County Court House to set county policy and to collect and disburse public funds. It relies on an elected county sheriff to enforce its orders. The court's tax mission is overseen by an elected county tax assessor and an appointed payroll tax administrator.

The court's membership comes from all the county's communities. South Shiloh contributes two magistrates, the Landing contributes one magistrate and two successive county judges, and Clarksville contributes one magistrate and the county clerk. In conducting county business, these men represent not only their constituents, but also their respective families, neighborhoods, religions, and communities. Baptists, Catholics, and Methodists all serve, as do both Democrats and Republicans.

Setting a Goal

Shiloh's record of industrialization is impressive: the county attracted nearly $300 million worth of industrial facilities between 1955 and 1970. A few employment figures illustrate how dramatic Shiloh's industrialization was: whereas in 1958 the county had only six industrial jobs, by 1970 industry supported 2,203 employees. What had been a rural county with a declining agricultural economy was becoming an industrial center.

Rural industrialization does not automatically lead to developmental change. In fact, Summers has found that rural industrialization can "exacerbate the very conditions it was supposed to have relieved."[5] In order to attract industry, the communities Summers studied had to offer inducements – usually services such as police and fire protection, water and sewage facilities, and road maintenance. The demand for these services exceeded the communities' capacity to provide them. Shiloh offered industry none of these services because the county had nothing even remotely equal to industry's needs. Instead, the county offered municipal industrial bonds and a "good attitude" toward business as inducements. Shiloh thus escaped one potential set of problems in its industrialization process.

However, three other problems mentioned by Summers were overwhelming Shiloh by 1970. The first was "payroll leakage." A 1969 survey showed that only 30 percent of the county's work force lived within the county. The other 70 percent lived within a thirty-mile radius of the factories, preferring to commute rather than live in an area with inadequate housing, no planned recreational facilities, and a comparatively poor educational system.

A second problem besetting the rural communities that Summers studied was a low multiplier effect (the factor which makes the local income resulting from investment in an area greater than the amount of the original investment). Private business growth was not spurred in Shiloh. The problem was not simply that 70 percent of the industrial payroll left the county; a good part of the remaining 30 percent was also spent in the larger stores of nearby urban areas. Thus, while the factories flourished, local business remained in the doldrums.

The third problem was "the inability of local governments to convert growth in the private sector into public revenue."[6] Some of the industries in Shiloh were on local tax rolls, but the major ones – $200 million worth – were protected from local taxation by virtue of being the nominal property of local governments. They were thus immune to paying taxes that would, in turn, further support programs of developmental change.

To compound these problems, industrialization attracted 1,750 new residents between 1960 and 1970. The newcomers built homes that contributed to the county's tax revenue, but the contribution was minor compared to the strain that the additional residents placed upon Shiloh's inadequate services. Although the fiscal court tried to solve the problem by setting property taxes at the highest rate allowed by state law, services still fell short of demand.

This, then, was the county's situation as it entered the 1970s. Industrialization had occurred but was not enriching the county's business or political establishments, since industrial employees commuted and industry was exempt from local taxation. The people who settled in Shiloh because of industrialization contributed to public revenues, but their tax money was inadequate to fund additional services. County residents were bitter. They had supported industrialization because it was a potential cure for Shiloh's problems. They had been promised that new plants would attract 25,000 new residents. Instead, fewer than 2,000 newcomers settled in Shiloh. This led one man to say, "We got raped. What we want are good middle-class people. That sounds like hell, but you know what I mean."

County dissatisfaction weighed heavily upon the fiscal court. The people wanted industrialization to finance the kinds of developmental change that would attract rather than repel people. And this became Shiloh's goal.

Setting Priorities and Imposing a Payroll Tax

The task of setting priorities for developmental change was complicated by the fiscal court's internal politics. The magistrates, county clerk, and county tax assessor were opposed to Judge Bass's leadership. Decision making, therefore, was keyed to both the politics of developmental change and the politics of succession. Both political agendas figured in the court's deliberations on imposing a 1-percent payroll tax.

Shiloh's authority to impose a payroll tax was a consequence of a state law known as "Home Rule," which reversed state policy toward local political subdivisions. From the time of its admission to the Union until 1971, the state had authority in most issues, and local political subdivisions had only those powers specifically granted to them by state law. The new Home Rule granted them all those powers not specifically reserved for federal and state governments. One of the powers granted to local political subdivisions was the right to impose a one-percent payroll tax. If such a tax were imposed in Shiloh County, it would generate about $400,000 per year and cause federal revenue sharing to increase by about $100 000 per year. The total revenue of $500,000 would double the county's budget and, because the money was not restricted to specific accounts, would allow the fiscal court to address local problems without interference.

Imposing a payroll tax would transform one of industrialization's drawbacks, a commuting work force, into a source of public revenue to finance programs of developmental change. A July article in the *Shiloh Crier* defined the county's fiscal plight. The Shiloh County Chamber of Commerce sent a delegation of officers to a regular fiscal court meeting to lobby for the tax. "We provide jobs, but we are unable to provide services," observed the chamber's president. The vice president proferred the payroll tax as the solution, one that would allow the court to make "a county we'll be proud of. Let's make Shiloh County the number one county in the state." The Clarksville magistrate acknowledged local support for the measure: "I was asked four years ago to favor a payroll tax. In fact, there wasn't a law authorizing such a tax at that time."

The court's new authority led to public hearings. These were held in the circuit court room of the Shiloh County Court House on two different evenings. Each hearing started with a definition of the payroll tax ("A fee for the privilege of engaging in any occupation or trade in the county") and a statement of the purposes of the hearings (to inform the public and to listen to the advice of citizens). Judge Bass noted that the hearings were not required by law but were attempts to gain citizen counsel. "We don't want to ram this thing down your throats," he said.

The county attorney presented a rationale for the tax. "There are certain pressing needs in the county. To meet these needs, there is a need for more money." Specifically, the fiscal court wanted to (1) provide adequate ambulance service; (2) do something about the rundown condition of the county court house; (3) improve the county's roads; (4) introduce a recreation program; (5) develop new water and sewer districts; (6) improve the garbage disposal system; and (7) bring landfill facilities into compliance with state law.

The communities' different interests led to an immediate dispute over priorities. The Clarksville magistrate said that the most pressing needs were adequate ambulance service, the court house, and roads. A South Shiloh magistrate disagreed: "My number one concern is roads. People in my district don't have any paved roads." He also argued that payroll tax money should be allocated equally among magisterial districts, regardless of population; the second South Shiloh magistrate supported this position.

Disputes on spending priorities were not the only disagreements voiced at the meetings. Participants were generally split into two competing groups. One group, composed of businessmen and city politicians, favored the tax and the services it could provide. The second group was composed of farmers and wage earners who opposed the tax. One lifelong resident contrasted the two groups, saying, "The further you get from the court house, the greater the opposition."

The clash led supporters of the tax to couch arguments in terms of exploiting external sources to meet local needs. A Landing politician said, "Either we get some money from outside Shiloh County to help pay for our needs or Shiloh County citizens will have to pay for it alone." This was seconded by another Landing politician, who said, "The people who have been citizens of the county all of our lives and new residents are going to ask for the services. It comes to the question whether we are going to pay for all of the services or whether they are going to help us." The Clarksville magistrate preferred the latter: "This is the cheapest way to get the money. If it doesn't happen this way, it's going to have to be done another."

Those opposed to the tax phrased their opposition in terms of equity: the payroll tax was unfair because it taxed wage earners the most, self-employed the least, and plants not at all. "Why is the man who brings home the paycheck at the top of the list?" asked a wage earner.

The county attorney explained that federal law made it illegal to tax the gross earnings of the self-employed. As for plants, the Clarksville magistrate pointed out, "To tax them would be to kill the goose that laid the golden egg. We don't want to make this area unattractive for future industrial development."

"A small farm can't afford to show a profit," a hill farmer complained; he assured the court that his would not. Another small farmer phrased the argument more eloquently: "I'll take care of myself. Why can't everybody else?"

The court was not swayed by equity arguments, and the opposition, led by Judge Bass's son-in-law, began to question motives. Where were the proposed water and sewer districts going? Whose land would be serviced? Who would profit? There was a hint of skullduggery here.

The Clarksville magistrate resented questioning of the court's integrity. "If you don't like what we're doing, vote us out of office in the next election and put someone in who will repeal the payroll tax." The opposition promised to do so.

A member of the audience stood and asked the members of the court about constituent support for the tax. Magistrates from the Landing and Clarksville said that their districts were in favor; the magistrates from South Shiloh refused to answer. Judge Bass was pressed to give his reading of voter sentiment. "I don't think that's a fair question to ask me," he said. After repeated calls, he responded, "Of all the people I've talked with, the majority were either for or against it."

Cuba Landing politicians claimed that Judge Bass "is afraid of it" because of the impending election. While none of the magistrates had election opponents, Judge Bass faced Frank Henry. Since the payroll tax was controversial, any action on the judge's part would affect election results. Landing politicians speculated that Judge Bass had planted his son-in-law in the audience to speak against the tax and thereby delay its imposition.

Shiloh's communal frames of reference came into full play in the next regular meeting of the court. At a premeeting caucus all members agreed not to consider the tax until after the election; with that issue settled, the regular meeting was convened. However, the court's magistrates were opposed to Judge Bass's reelection and were willing to use the payroll tax to damage the Judge's election chances. A magistrate with familial, neighborhood, religious, community, and partisan political affiliations that differed from those of Judge Bass moved to impose a 1-percent payroll tax. Clarksville and Landing magistrates voted in favor of the motion, and the two South Shiloh magistrates abstained. Judge Bass, as the fifth voting member of the court, had to cast the deciding ballot. The vote was three to zero in favor. "It was politics. There was an election coming up, don't you see?" explained the judge.

The election campaign turned the court's proceedings into a political theater with all arguments and decisions being made to influence voters. This was illustrated in the two meetings immediately preceding elections. Neither meeting had a formal agenda, and the court addressed issues on the basis of delegation complaint, political expediency, and the lung power of participants.

Typical of court proceedings prior to elections was the way that Judge Bass handled a delegation of neighbors from Phillips in South Shiloh concerned with paving a road. The neighbors approached the court en masse, and the session broke down into a set of private discussions between magistrates and delegation members. The road was pointed out on a map, and Judge Bass said that it was too late to pave it that year but that it would be paved the next year. The delegation recognized this promise as mere political expendiency to influence their votes.

The same expediency was demonstrated when the group of neighbors prepared to leave. A South Shiloh magistrate asked the delegation to stay longer and discuss ambulance service. They did so and suggested several changes in the magistrate's plan. Judge Bass left the room, then returned. Saying that the magistrate's plan discriminated against Phillips, he pledged to fight his court to gain equity for South Shiloh.

Similarly, expediency surfaced when Judge Bass admitted that he had hired a man to work for the county road department without prior court approval, despite a resolution that called for court concurrence in new hirings. A magistrate noted that it was October and road work lessened in the winter. Another magistrate pointed out that the appointee had a large kinship group, many members of which were registered voters. The judge's actions led to a discussion about hiring policy. The county road supervisor said that he needed men experienced in using heavy equipment, not more shovelers. The Clarksville magistrate asked, "Would you be willing to hire and fire?"

"Uh uh. I've got too many enemies on this job already." Speaking of his employees, he added, "All of these folks are my friends."

"I've never hired one yet," Judge Bass said in defense of his hiring practices.

"You just did," said a magistrate.

"And I didn't get him on," said the judge.

The discussion then turned to paving in Buck Snort. Two bids were opened. The county had advertised for one-and-a-half-inches of blacktop, whereas the bids specified two inches. Judge Bass left the meeting and returned a little later. He said that both firms had agreed to lower their bids by one-quarter for one-and-a-half-inch blacktop. The county attorney objected on the grounds that it was illegal to accept bids over the telephone. Judge Bass countered. He asked a magistrate to make a motion to accept the telephone bids; the magistrate did not. The court decided to advertise for bids once again, and the meeting ended.

A *Shiloh Crier* reporter put the Buck Snort paving issue into perspective. "We all know what that's about," he said. The Judge had struck a deal: paved streets in return for votes. However, Frank Henry had made an issue of one-and-a-half-inch blacktop, saying publicly that it was little better than a paint stripe. Judge Bass responded by altering bid specifications. In the words of the Clarksville magistrate, "It's all political."

Another set of actions based on political expediency surfaced in the last regular fiscal court meeting prior to the election. At issue were the ethics of accepting a HUD grant that would allow the court to purchase Pine Wood Park, a ninety-one-acre parcel of land south of Clarksville that included a thirty-five-acre lake. HUD had offered the court a grant that would pay 50 percent of the purchase price, or $41,000, whichever was less. The court had hired an out-of-county realtor to appraise the land. His figure was $77,000. The current owners, who were county residents, had offered to sell for less so that the excess HUD money could be returned to the county for site development. Judge Bass was in favor of the appraisal reimbursement arrangement because it would allow him to face the county's voters as a man "who brought things into the county."

During discussion the judge left the meeting room and returned with a fly swatter. He swung at a fly on the table and missed. A magistrate expressed a need for caution about the legality of the judge's site purchase plan. Judge Bass leaned under the table to swat two flies on the county attorney's leg.

"You missed, Judge," said the county attorney.

"No I didn't."

A swatted fly took wing.

"Look at that sucker go," said Judge Bass.

The Clarksville magistrate said that he had contracted HUD for advice. HUD wanted the court to send a letter saying that the land was appraised for $77,000 but that the sellers were willing to transfer title for less.

"At least it won't be crooked," said a South Shiloh magistrate.

"If it's a skeleton, there's a hell of a lot of skeletons walking around," said Judge Bass.

"But they're in somebody else's house," said a magistrate.

The court refused to accept the judge's appraisal/reimbursement scheme, and Judge Bass had to face the voters without Pine Wood Park. Frank Henry won the election by a forty-eight-vote margin. The county had ratified the magistrates' decision that the fiscal court needed new leadership.

Judge Henry was installed, and his first court meeting witnessed a change of style. Gone was the "meeting-of-peers" format, and in its place Judge Henry sat at the head of the table and held business to an orderly flow with the aid of a printed agenda and a gavel. Judge Henry was also skilled at attracting various programs. He used his expertise whenever possible because, as he said, "If the money isn't spent in Shiloh County, it'll be spilled in the gutters of Brooklyn." The court was thus ready to recommence its programs of developmental change.

Meeting Goals

Ambulance Service. Shiloh's ambulance service was maintained by funeral directors in Clarksville and the Landing. When new state and federal laws required improved equipment and personnel, the funeral directors could not meet these requirements. During the election campaign for county judge, they proposed not to renew their contracts.

The proposal put the court in a difficult position. Shiloh needed ambulance service but could have it only by subsidizing the funeral directors. The fiscal court was the only agency that could guarantee the money because, according to the Clarksville magistrate in an article in the *Shiloh Crier,* "From a financial standpoint we cannot turn to the two cities for assistance." But a subsidy from the court would support private, profit-making businesses – a practice that many of Shiloh's voters condemned.

Ambulance service problems were debated throughout the fall. During the meeting immediately preceding the election, the court tried to settle the issue by agreeing to limit the contract and ambulance franchise to a one-year term. Judge Bass objected. "It ain't gonna do it, boys. The one-year franchise is no good."

"All they can have, Judge, is a one-year contract," answered a magistrate.

The court advertised for bids. The only bid was for $78,000 for one year's service; it was rejected. As of the new year, Shiloh would be without ambulance service unless something was done.

Fortunately, something was done. In December the *Shiloh Crier* carried a front page story headlined "Funeral Homes Contract to End Ambulance Search." The funeral homes agreed to provide service for a one-year period provided the court would finance the purchase of needed equipment. The story concluded, "The fiscal court has battled with the problem of ambulance service for many monthly meetings and was almost stymied in its efforts until the two directors voiced a renewed interest in the service." The immediate crisis was met, but its cause – new legal requirements – remained.

Ambulance problems were emphasized by a delegation complaint to the court. A man had nearly died in Phillips because an out-of-county ambulance from Cade's Hollow had refused to enter Shiloh on the grounds that to do so would make the ambulance service liable to legal action for violating the ambulance franchise. A magistrate complained, "There's no restriction whatsoever on who can come into Shiloh County."

The delegation spokesman said that people in Phillips used the same telephone exchange, markets, and community services as their neighbors in Cade's Hollow. Furthermore, drivers from Cade's Hollow did not get lost in South Shiloh, as did drivers from Clarksville and the Landing. "We'uns six miles from Cade's Hollow. Hit's our best," said the delegation spokesman. The court agreed to write a letter stating that South Shiloh fell under no franchise agreement and that the Cade's Hollow service should render aid as requested.

A better solution began to take shape when Judge Henry invited a member of the regional health planning council to tell the court about new federal grants. "It's a whole new ball game as far as we're concerned."

As it was explained to the court, the council had a federal grant. If the court would furnish some idea of the county's health needs, the council would draw up a plan with an eye toward using federal assistance to meet those needs. A funeral director immediately spoke of the problems of maintaining ambulance services. "It all boils down to the fact that they are asking more requirements in 1975 than they did in 1974."

The new requirements placed the funeral directors in legal jeopardy. "We put seventy-two hours in the classroom last year," said a director, yet ambulance personnel were still not fully qualified. Judge Henry, who presided over the civil court, reassured the director. "I don't feel you could get a civil conviction in any court in Shiloh County and you certainly won't have any legal problems with the fiscal court."

"There are other ways and there is money available," said the council representative. A 75-percent federal grant could be obtained to purchase equipment and train personnel. "This is the time to get the money," said the council representative. "The money is there. Those that take advantage of it are going to get it and when it's gone, it's gone – like any other federal money. If we can get a 75-percent grant, we'd better be thinking seriously about getting it," said Judge Henry.

Agreeing to use payroll tax funds as seed money to provide the county's 25 percent, the court decided to apply for the grant.

The funeral director and the council representative left the meeting, and the fiscal court reviewed the problem. Neighboring county governments paid up to $80,000 per year for ambulance services. Shiloh paid $24,000. The federal grant would finance new equipment without much cost to the court and without alienating the funeral directors. The funeral directors were seen as key figures in providing Shiloh's ambulance service. The Clarksville magistrate summarized court opinion, saying, "I think we should proceed with extreme caution. If we don't we're going to have one hell of a problem." But problems were successfully avoided: Shiloh's application for a grant to finance new ambulances that would meet state and federal legal requirements was accepted.

The court considered installing a countywide radio dispatching system to supplement the ambulance service. A central radio would be located in the sheriff's office and used to direct police, fire, and ambulance services. During a specially called court meeting the judge was authorized to apply for a 100-percent grant of $17,000 to pay the salaries of three dispatchers. In another meeting the court approved a bid of $20,452.03 for communications equipment. The court, under Judge Henry's leadership, had thus solved two local problems.

The County Court House. The Shiloh County Court House, which was built in 1865, was in poor repair. The court had been diverting maintenance funds to meet other expenditures for "at least the last thirty-three years," according to an expert witness. Yet one magistrate remarked, "I've been a member of the Fiscal Court for three and one-half years and every time the grand jury has returned a report to the court, the number one priority has been the court house."

While most people agreed that the condition of the court house was a problem, there was no agreement on a possible solution. Two factions formed within the body politic during debate. One faction advocated tearing down the court house and replacing it with a new structure, arguing that a modern building would be a fitting symbol for a new county, one which was competitive with others in the area. The other faction said that the court house was a historic landmark, symbolic of Shiloh's heritage; to destroy the building would be to destroy much of the county's traditions.

Broadly speaking, the two factions represented Shiloh's north-south split. One resident said that the closer one was to the court house, the greater one's desire to see it replaced. The split in Shiloh's body politic posed problems for Judge Henry's future political ambitions. He said he wanted to use his present office as a stepping stone into the state legislature and, ultimately, into the governor's mansion. He thus had to gauge the effect of present decisions on future plans. The advice he received was not helpful. An outside observer suggested that the greatest political advantage would accrue to those who, despite blind and prejudiced opposition, built a new structure. Observers closer to Shiloh said the greatest political advantage would accrue to those who, despite blind and prejudiced opposition, renovated the old structure.

The magistrates mirrored the split in the body politic and it looked like the debate would end in permanent factionalism, broken only by Judge Henry's deciding vote. Then Judge Henry found a way to finesse the problem: HUD had $8 million to aid rural counties and towns in the state that were interested in improving blighted areas and restoring historic buildings. "We can get 100 percent money for the historic preservation of this building. This is available. You can't get any of this money to build a new court house. It's for anything you want to restore to its original appearance," Judge Henry explained to the court.

"It's crazy. The federal government is crazy," said an opposing member of the court.

Crazy or not, the court held a public hearing. Judge Henry told the audience that he had attended a HUD-sponsored seminar to learn more about the program:

> I'm hopeful that what I found out will have some effect on the court's decision. HUD set certain guidelines on how this money may be spent. And when you read the guidelines, you think someone must have been thinking about Shiloh County. We're talking about absolutely no commitment. No money from Shiloh County. I'd like to be authorized to seek out this commercial development money. It will cost absolutely nothing to try.

"Let's go get it," urged a South Shiloh magistrate.

The Clarksville magistrate agreed but with reservations. "I would be in favor of trying to get this grant. But if the money is not available in the form of this grant, let's do away with this building."

There was little doubt that the grant would be forthcoming. Judge Henry explained that "Congressman Harb will help us if this is what we want to do." Congressman Harb sat on the committee that approved HUD's budget.

Political reckoning was borne out. Judge Henry told the court that the state's HUD representative was impressed with Shiloh's application. "His recommendation is that we submit a joint application with the City of Clarksville."

The joint application was filed. Then the court received a letter from HUD saying that, although Shiloh was eligible, the chances for approval were slim. Bureaucrats in HUD had intervened to favor applications from areas with high rates of unemployment; Shiloh's level of unemployment was comparatively low. Despite the discouraging response from HUD, the court agreed to continue the application process.

The application failed, and Shiloh's traditional political game, which pitted the power of rival community coalitions against one another, recommenced. As Judge Henry said in a meeting called to inform the public about the court house issue, "Some members of the court feel that this building should be maintained at all costs. There are others that feel it has served the county well for 110 years, [but it should now be replaced]." The only relevant question was which coalition had the power to force its preference on the other.

The meeting turned into a discussion between magistrates on the course to be taken. One group of magistrates wanted to replace the building. To justify their stance, they said that a new building would cost about $1,000,000, whereas renovation and construction of an annex would cost about $1,500,000. The other group of magistrates, mindful of tradition and the coalition within the court, rejected cost as the basis for decision making. "My mind is made up. These figures don't do too much for me," said a South Shiloh magistrate.

Judge Henry revealed the workings of the coalition within the court: "There is the possibility that the court might have two different opinions. I'd like to see the court be unanimous in our decision if that's at all possible. However, rather than have a split vote, I would not be hesitant to break the tie."

The Clarksville magistrate then made a motion to tear the court house down and replace it with a new structure, the Cuba Landing magistrate seconded the motion, and the county clerk called for the vote. Clarksville and Cuba Landing were in favor; the two magistrates from South Shiloh were opposed; and Judge Henry, contrary to his word, abstained. There were no further motions. The debate continued for another month.

Prior to the second meeting, the magistrates learned the opinions of their constituents. Clarksville businessmen wanted a new court house, and Judge Henry was publicly told by the president of the chamber of commerce that, while the chamber did not want to dictate solutions, it wanted a decision. As Judge Henry said when the second meeting was opened, "I think it's important before we leave here tonight that we come to a final decision."

Judge Henry mentioned a solution that his constituents had offered:

> I've been asked how I feel about putting this on the ballot. As far as I'm concerned, it would be a cop-out. It might be the easy way out, but I don't think the people elected us to take the easy way out. God knows I've tried to come up with a compromise. But if we can't come up with a compromise, let's do what the people elected us to do.

A South Shiloh magistrate offered a mock compromise. "Build it where the town's going to be. Back to the south or southeast. You need pontoons here." The compromise was not acceptable.

"It's very important for downtown Clarksville to stay alive. The court house has to remain. I will never cast my vote to move the court house," declared the Clarksville magistrate.

"I feel the same way about moving the court house as I do about tearing this court house down. This court house is right where it ought to be," said Judge Henry.

"I want to save this building," said a South Shiloh magistrate.

"It looks like the cards are on the table. We're split. I'd just like for us to do something, right or wrong," said the Clarksville magistrate.

"What's the feeling of the court?" asked Judge Henry.

"I'll make a motion to preserve this building and go across the street to build an annex," said a South Shiloh magistrate. The second magistrate from South Shiloh seconded the motion, and the vote was taken. Clarksville and Cuba Landing were opposed; South Shiloh was in favor. Judge Henry cast the final ballot in favor of the motion. The working majority had succeeded to the astonishment of regular court observers, one of whom told his fellow Court House Square loafers the next morning, "That whippersnapper from the Landing surprised all of us."

But the final word came from the floor during debate. "Build a court house. Build an annex. But save something to build roads," cautioned a member of the audience.

Roads. The imposition of a payroll tax, the election of a county judge, and the ambulance service decision were examples of Shiloh's magistrates acting more or less in agreement. In the debate over the county court house, Judge Henry's attempts to maintain a working majority in the court allied him with South Shiloh's two magistrates. They supported his ambitions for the court house in return for his support for paving roads in their areas. The South Shiloh-county judge coalition was effective largely because it was not widely recognized for some time.

Thus, the decision to renovate the court house and build an annex across the street was part of a larger political agenda within the fiscal court. The logrolling started another political exchange that ended when the Shiloh County Chamber of Commerce allied itself with the Cuba Landing City Council in petitioning for magisterial redistricting. By invoking the provisions of the Supreme Court's one-man, one-vote ruling, they sought to break the court coalition to pave roads in South Shiloh and achieve a more equitable distribution of payroll tax monies. Shiloh's magisterial districts were created in 1850 and had not been changed for 126 years (see Figure 2). They might have remained unaltered for another 126 years, but the knowledge that South Shiloh and Judge Henry controlled the court, and thus the distribution of the new payroll tax funds, prompted the chamber and the Landing to take action. Neither organization was willing to allow 22 percent of Shiloh's population to set policy and priorities for county government, particularly when South Shiloh's magistrates had not supported the payroll tax.

Petitioning, the last activity of the Chamber-Landing alliance, came late because roads had not been viewed as part of coalition politics. The state, the court, and the county's residents all held that Shiloh's roads were grossly inadequate because of a shortage of both equipment and materials. The court had purchased some equipment with federal revenue-sharing money, but revenue sharing was an uncertain source of funds because it depended on unpredictable congressional action. The court felt that the best course was to invest these funds in equipment and not in continuing projects so that, if the revenue-sharing program ended, Shiloh would retain its funds in the form of graders and bulldozers.

The linkage between Shiloh's roads and federal programs was also uncertain. A project calling for federal money to modernize a U.S. highway between the Landing and Clarksville revealed the frustrations of dealing with the federal government. A state highway

Figure 2
Shiloh's Magisterial Redistricting Map

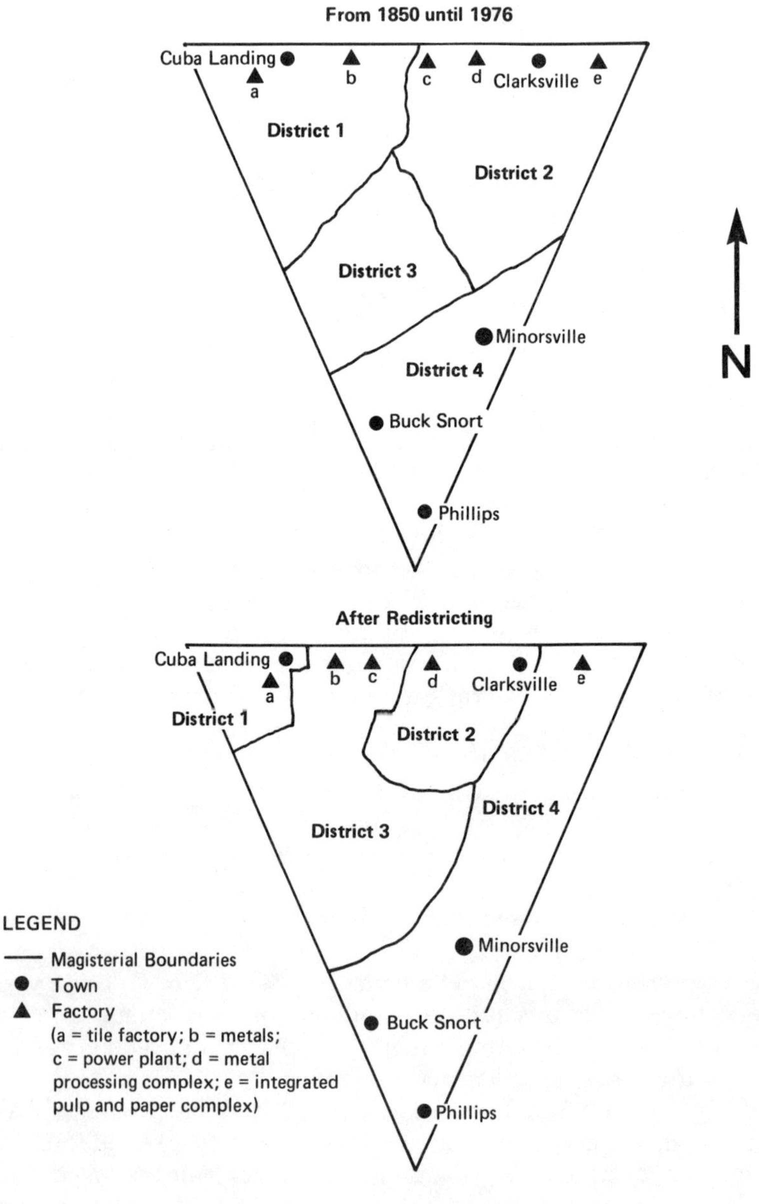

engineer said in August, "We've been through the design stage three times and it's still not complete . . . . Finances have been a major holdup . . . federal highway legislation has been rejected by Congress for the past two years and without it the state's financial burden is phenomenal."

On February 28, 1974, a delegation of Shiloh citizens traveled to the state capital and heard their governor announce that the problem was solved: federal funds were available to make the road a four-lane highway. The funds allowed the governor to keep his campaign pledge to modernize the highway.

After the governor's public announcement to the delegation, Judge Henry asked about several other appeals that he had made. "Don't try to kill all the chickens in the coop in the first six months, Judge. It can't be done," said the governor.

Judge Henry thought differently. As he told one of his political confidants, he had eleven requests on the governor's desk "and he's approved three of them."

"Three out of eleven ain't bad," said the friend.

Shortly after the meeting with the governor, the state started surveying the road and thereafter state agents purchased property on the right-of-way and helped relocate affected residents. The new highway started to take shape.

Another road program showed more certain linkage between Shiloh and outside agencies. The state's department of highways was charged by state law with maintaining certain roads in all rural counties. A delegation from the highway department met with the court to explain two state highway programs.

The court learned that there were sixty-eight miles of gravel/mud road and sixty miles of blacktop eligible for state aid, and the state could not set maintenance priorities. "We don't have any authority to tell you what to do on any county road," said a member of the state's delegation.

Local control of state road programs was apparent in the delegation's request that the court set priorities. During the discussion a delegation member said that a South Shiloh resident had written the department requesting improvement of one road. A magistrate objected to the request. "Four years ago you couldn't drive over it with a tractor. Now you can take a Cadillac over it." The resident's request was denied by the court.

A South Shiloh magistrate asked if maintenance requirements on gravel roads could be lowered and the savings used to maintain blacktop roads. This could be done, but the delegation cautioned: "Sixty miles of blacktop and you've created a monster."

Blacktop was called a "monster" because neither the state nor the county could afford more than major bituminous highways supplemented by gravel roads. A gravel road could always be recovered from natural ravage, but a blacktop road could be lost. Also, a blacktop road needed repaving every seven years; a gravel road required only minor maintenance. Finally, it cost $20,000 per mile to resurface blacktop and $30,000 per mile to build new bituminous surfaces. There was not enough money to create and care for paved roads.

The court agreed on a set of measures. State funds would be used to replace a bridge. The court would lower gravel specifications from eighty to sixty tons per mile and would use the savings to purchase more blacktop patching. Although the court, in particular the South Shiloh magistrates, saw this as a less-than-perfect set of choices, the opportunities afforded by state resources were limited.

In the same meeting John Horn, the realtor/builder who opposed Bob Robbins in the Cuba Landing City Council, approached the court with a road problem. A private road serviced his subdivision, and his bank refused to lend more building money unless local government assumed maintenance costs.

"What has been the court's policy in the past?" asked Judge Henry. It had been confused. One thing, however, stood out: gravel roads were sometimes accepted, but paved roads never were, and Horn's road was blacktopped.

"What's the decision of the court?" asked Judge Henry.

"Let's talk about it," said a magistrate. In the end, Cuba Landing took responsibility for the road.

Judge Henry nearly finessed road problems and the petition for magisterial district reapportionment with a change in Shiloh's road tax legislation. Shiloh's voters had supported a road maintenance tax of $.13 per $100 assessed property valuation, but state law required periodic voter approval of the tax. Judge Henry persuaded the fiscal court to recommend continuance of the tax with one change. Rather than having tax money finance road maintenance, the funds would go to new road and bridge construction. The public rationale was that a countywide tax would help those in greatest need. Judge Henry phrased his request in terms of neighboring. "If the people in Shiloh County want good roads, want their neighbors to have good roads, then they have the opportunity," he said. The private rationale for the tax was that the unencumbered funds would be used to blacktop roads in South Shiloh. This would free payroll tax money for other purposes and still maintain Judge Henry's three-vote majority in the fiscal court.

The court held public meetings on the tax issue. The public rationale of neighboring was swept aside by Shiloh's insistence that neighbors live in close association with one another.

"Will any of the proceeds go to city streets?" asked Clarksville's Mayor Harold.

"I cannot say they would not," said Judge Henry.

"I'm a little disappointed if some money isn't allocated because we're paying $.13 like people in the back end of the county. Do you think, based on the amount of taxes paid, people in the city are getting back what the people in the back of the county are getting?" asked Mayor Harold.

"It's going to be my position that the money be spent in as equitable a manner as possible," said Judge Henry. He touched on the idea of neighboring again. "I think the majority of people in Shiloh have always tried to help one another." But the voters disagreed with Judge Henry's expanded idea of neighboring and defeated the proposed tax by a 111-vote margin.

The payroll tax money would have to be used to meet South Shiloh's demands for more blacktopped roads. The court allocated $250,000 to construct eight miles of paved roads. Each magisterial district gained two miles of new paving, an arrangement that favored South Shiloh because 50 percent of the appropriation benefitted only 22 percent of the population.

Inequitable distribution of payroll tax monies stirred local debate. Those who had supported the payroll tax were opposed to road construction; they wanted the money spent on services that would attract new residents. But the court's coalition frustrated their wishes. Thus, the Shiloh County Chamber of Commerce and the Cuba Landing City Council seized upon the Supreme Court's one-man, one-vote ruling to petition for magisterial redistricting. And even here they were partly frustrated, for reapportionment took time. Until the next elections the coalition in the court would stand. "They can't do a thing about it for two years and five months [when new elections would bring new magistrates to the court]," said a member of the coalition.

Recreation. Shiloh's recreational program nearly broke the court's coalition because it spent money that some of the coalition members would have used to build roads. South Shiloh's residents said they wanted roads, not the services that would attract new residents into North Shiloh. A South Shiloh magistrate echoed his constituents' wishes when he said, "I've lived in mud all my life." Neither he nor his constituents intended to die in mud. They wanted surfaced, all-weather roads.

The near rupture in the court's coalition followed a long history of seeking developmental change in recreation. The court and the schools had offered a jointly sponsored program for the county's youth. The court supplied funds for the hiring of recreational directors and the schools supplied facilities and buses. But the program died because the court could not locate stable funding.

Finally, the court located a HUD grant that would make possible the purchase of Pine Wood as a site for a county park. Pine Wood was owned by two Clarksville businessmen. Its purchase hinged on HUD's signals to the court, the purchase price, the politics in the county judge election, and the court's attempts to gain clear title to three lots within the park's boundaries. After Judge Henry's appraisal/reimbursement scheme was rebuffed by a majority of the fiscal court, and after he failed in his bid for reelection, a member of the court paid an option price from his own pocket in order to gain clear title to the lots. Once the court reimbursed him, the county owned Pine Wood.

The court's planned recreational program was enhanced when the U.S. Bureau of Outdoor Recreation approved grants for small parks in South Shiloh and Clarksville. The South Shiloh Park was developed independently, but the Clarksville Park was incorporated with Pine Wood. The court authorized $200,000 to develop the parks. South Shiloh gained a baseball diamond while Pine Wood gained a road, a bath house, a swimming area, two baseball diamonds, tennis courts, picnic areas, and a children's playground.

The court's coalition was strained when people from South Shiloh objected to park development in lieu of road construction and residents of the Clarksville-Cuba Landing area criticized the court for spending money on roads rather than on the services that would attract new residents. This countywide debate further supported the petition to reorganize the court's magisterial districts.

Water Districts and Garbage Disposal. Many of the county's other needs were also met. A new water district, financed by federal grants and loans, extended an existing system into South Shiloh. Garbage disposal and a solid waste program were also instituted. By mid-1976 Judge Henry said that the county had moved from a building phase to a maintenance phase; no one publicly disagreed with him.

DEVELOPMENTAL CHANGE AND IMPOSED SYSTEMIC LINKAGES

The fiscal court's activities show that local decisions, or politics, are responsible for Shiloh's developmental change, or planned changes in facilities and services. Shiloh's response to externally imposed systemic linkages is illustrated by the role of the Shiloh County Planning and Zoning Commission.

The commission was formed as a result of federal initiative. Both the Landing and Clarksville had traditionally discharged raw sewage into the river. The federal Environmental Protection Agency warned that continued discharge was against federal law and the cities stood in legal jeopardy. The cities said they knew they were violating the law, but they were financially unable to do otherwise. The Environmental Protection Agency said that funds were available to construct sewage treatment plants in both cities, provided that Cuba Landing and Clarksville make joint application for the money and that all three local governments jointly participate in land use planning.

The bargain was struck: both cities installed sewage treatment plants with federal funds and all three units of local government applied for and received a HUD grant for a land use study. The study document, *Shiloh County: The Comprehensive Plan,* listed rules governing land use and created the Shiloh County Planning and Zoning Commission to enforce them. The commission was systemically linked to HUD through an intermediary agency, the Area Development District, whose representatives regularly attended commission meetings.

Shiloh's communal frames of reference intervened in the commission's activities from the start. South Shiloh refused to participate in land use planning. Since South Shiloh was not getting a sewage treatment plant, there was no political leverage to force the area to join the commission. So the commission's mandate, sanctioned by state law, was formally defined as ensuring that desirable development occurred in the magisterial districts comprising the Cuba Landing-Clarksville area, rather than throughout the county. Achieving desirable development was publicly defined as acquiring urban amenities without adding urban woes to the county's problems. "The purpose of a planning and zoning commission is to make the county a place people can be proud of," as a representative of the Area Development District explained to the commission. Privately, the commission's mandate was defined according to Shiloh's communal frames of reference and the political processes these generated.

The private definition of power came about because the commission was under local control, despite its origin, mandate, legal sanction, and systemic linkage with HUD through the Area Development District. Local control of the commission was exercised in three ways. First, city and county governments appointed commission members. Second, city and county governments had the power to accept or reject zoning decisions. This made the commission a recommending body, as its chairman explained during a visit to the Clarksville City Council:

> The planning and zoning commission is purely an advisory group. Any rezoning we have done in the past, you can overrule. It is really up to the city council to vote to approve or disapprove the rulings.

Third, local governments had financial control of the commission because they supplied most of the commission's budget.

These three factors meant that the commission's chairman was subject to a good deal of local advice and pressure with respect to how the commission should be run, thus making the chairmanship a less than desirable office. When new leadership was needed in 1974, commission members surveyed those present and nominated an absent member. A member then recommended that nominations be closed and the nominee be recognized as chairman. "That's the way to go, baby. You swept that one," said the Area Development District representative. When this new chairman resigned, another was chosen in the same way. As the *Shiloh Crier* reported in February 1976, the winning candidate "was not present during the nomination and balloting."

To fulfill its mandate, the commission, all of whose members were local people, made decisions that angered many applicants, some of whom were also local. Communal frames of reference were frequently in opposition to commission actions.

The use of communal frames of reference was evident in one zoning application. Two local men had asked the commission to approve plans for a subdivision. The request was denied: zoning regulations called for paved roads, and the subdivision planned a gravel road. The applicants argued that paving costs would kill the project and suggested that the fiscal court would maintain the road if the commission would accept their application.

The men then approached the fiscal court. A magistrate objected, "We're setting precedents. We're not just deciding one case. We're going to have to live with this from now on." Judge Bass demurred. The subdivision would help make Shiloh a better place to live. "Way I see it, we're setting a precedent. But we want the county to grow, don't we?"

The court agreed to accept maintenance responsibility provided the road was built to county specifications. The commission agreed to the proposed subdivision because it had been overruled. Local observers noted that both public and private considerations were factors in the court's decision. Judge Bass could publicly advocate acceptance because the subdivision helped Shiloh. It was not publicly noted, however, that one applicant was active in the judge's political party and the other was influential in determining the news coverage of the judge's election campaign.

Shiloh residents routinely used communal frames of reference to countermand commission rulings. When an application to alter a lot's status from single dwelling to commercial was denied, the applicant told the commission, "I want that land to become commercial. I'm going to keep after it until it does . . . . " A commission member countered. He told of a neighbor's vow "that if we passed it here, she'd take it to the city council." The commission gave conditional approval and let the neighbor take her case to the city council. However, the applicant was influential in Shiloh's Democratic Party and thus had political leverage. The applicant won the council's approval.

This pattern of accommodation to Shiloh's communal frames of reference influenced all the commission's decisions. One meeting dealt with a congregation that was building a church without a building permit. While the construction was in violation of land use rules, the commission chairman appreciated the power of religion in Shiloh: "I don't want to be facetious, but I'm not going to take on either the church or God." The commission took no action on the church's violation of land use regulations.

Such decisions symbolize the power of Shiloh's political processes as variables intervening in systemic linkages. The symbolic interaction led to the formation of divergent attitudes toward the commission. People not subject to Shiloh's political processes said the commission fulfilled its mandate. The Area Development District representative asked the commission for permission to bring members of a neighboring county's commission to visit a session. He said that Shiloh County's efforts were a beacon for other such bodies. "You all are in fine shape compared to the others."

Commission members, who were subject to Shiloh's political processes, did not share this view because they knew the reasons for commission decisions. One said that a fellow commission member had remodeled his house without the proper building permit. The member was not alone in his actions: other citizens ignored the commission. "You've had ordinances for five years and they aren't worth the paper they're written on."

The contention that the commission was powerless in the face of Shiloh's political processes brought prompt response from the Area Development District representative. "The thing about it is . . . just because you miss one, you can't let the rest ride. There has to be a place to start [enforcing land use regulations]." He nevertheless acknowledged the realities of decision making in Shiloh. "You can't go by the book 100 percent of the time because there are people involved."

Other commission members said that political circumvention of commission recommendations was justified. The document *Shiloh County: The Comprehensive Plan* was created by a nationally known research firm which was not familiar with the county. The document thus contained zoning maps that were not congruent with local priorities. The commission's recommendations, which were based on these maps, were in need of correction. "To hamper the growth of a town because of a map that is arbitrarily set up – that's ridiculous," observed one commission member.

The citizens adversely affected by the commission's recommendations shared the view that the commission made ridiculous recommendations. Their land was being policed and they did not want outside agencies tampering with personal property. As they said, the commission was attempting to make land use regulations intended for an urban setting applicable to a rural area. The regulations were, in this view, "way too strict."

Some of these feelings surfaced in a Clarksville City Council meeting when the commission chairman asked the council to approve its contribution to the commission's budget. The city's attorney opposed the request:

> I've been opposed to this thing from its very inception. This ordinance was brought about because the federal government told Clarksville and the Landing "no" on some grants unless we had a planning and zoning commission, among other things. The people of Shiloh County cannot live with this thing.

However, since Shiloh residents served as commission members and commission recommendations could be overruled by local governments whose decisions were shaped by Shiloh's political processes, the commission was responsive to local interests. Shiloh's political processes were thus capable of intervening in an externally imposed systemic linkage to represent and respond to local priorities.

Shiloh's industrialization and the workings of the fiscal court show the power of local autonomy in gaining developmental change. Moreover, the impotence of the Shiloh County Planning and Zoning Commission indicates the power of local autonomy to manipulate externally planned and imposed programs of developmental change. The narrative that follows shows local autonomy at work in Shiloh's quest for educational change.

Notes

1. Herriott and Hodgkins, *The Environment of Schooling,* p. 38.
2. Herbert F. Lionberger, *Adoption of New Ideas and Practices* (Ames, Iowa: University of Iowa Press, 1968), p. 93.
3. U.S. Congress, House, "Financing Private Industry by Tax-Free Municipal Bonds Should be Halted," *Congressional Record,* Feb. 15, 1967, pp. 3477-3479.
4. Surrey, Letter to Wilbur Mills, dated January 23, 1968.
5. Summers, "Small Towns Beware," p. 20.
6. Ibid.

Part 2

Education and Developmental Change in Shiloh

3

Introducing Developmental Change Into Shiloh's Schools

The foregoing account of fiscal court and planning and zoning commission operations shows how local political decisions determine changes in Shiloh County's facilities and services within the context of communal frames of reference (family, neighborhood, church, and community). Two modes of stimulating developmental change emerge from this account. The fiscal court responded to local needs and opinions by manipulating tax laws and using federal programs which could be targeted to local development and improvement. In contrast, the planning and zoning commission was an externally imposed advisory board. Although theoretically it could recommend regulations contrary to local interests, the commission was stymied by the political sophistication of Shiloh Countians who were able to promote local interests and still benefit from advantages offered by extralocal resources.

This distinction between the two processes which stimulated political and social change in Shiloh is essential for understanding the process of educational change that took place between 1971 and 1976. An inadequate rural educational system with minimal state accreditation quickly became eligible for membership in the Southern Association of Colleges and Schools, the highest accreditation in the region. The transformation fused local demands for developmental change in facilities with two external programs targeted to educational reform. As Shiloh began to transform its educational system, Congress was setting national educational policy to provide "every person an equal opportunity to receive an education of high quality."[1] One result of congressional interest in education was the creation of the Experimental Schools (ES) program. Under the aegis of national educational policy, the ES program proposed to demonstrate that programs of comprehensive educational change could be effective in altering fundamental individual and institutional behaviors in education.

The ES program was originally housed in the United States Office of Education, and its offerings were initially targeted to urban school districts. In 1972, shortly before being transferred from the Office of Education to the new National Institute of Education, the scope of the ES program was broadened to include rural school systems. Shiloh County was one of ten rural school districts chosen to receive funding for the implementation of planned, comprehensive, educational change.

The Shiloh County school system fashioned its program for comprehensive change after some of the recommendations contained in a survey of its schools which had been conducted by a nationally known research firm in response to political disputes over local priorities. Thus, the schools were responding simultaneously to local demands for educational development, to external recommendations for change, and to national educational policy.

The fusion of such disparate goals for change produced some complex situations, but certain consistent patterns emerged, particularly the use of local political processes to obtain external resources and manipulate externally imposed directives to local benefit.

The following four chapters describe the fusion of external and local change programs, the important role of Shiloh's superintendent of schools in introducing change to the schools, and the subsequent reactions of teachers and students. Some of Shiloh's needs for educational development, as the county defined them, were not met, an outcome that had consequences for the federal-local relationship.

BACKGROUND

The five members of the Shiloh County Board of Education are elected by members of families, neighborhoods, church congregations, and communities who demand that attention be given to local priorities. The strength of local demands in the board of education's decision making is evidenced by South Shiloh's response to state recommendations for school consolidation. In 1893 Shiloh had forty-six neighborhood schools. Emigration, all-weather roads, and state pressure for consolidation left the county with only four schools by 1970 – one consolidated high school and elementary centers in Buck Snort, Cuba Landing, and Clarksville. When the state department of education recommended consolidating Buck Snort with Clarksville, South Shiloh's two board members resisted the state's recommendations, and Buck Snort's school remained open.

Since the board of education is in the delicate position of having to balance state recommendations against local demands, its decisions are generally conservative. Only a major local issue can induce the board to deviate from this norm. Such deviation usually involves a long period of informal discussion among board members and constituents and trial ballots cast to reach an informal consensus before a decision is officially made on the basis of a majority vote.

The most telling illustration of this decision-making process involved the construction of two consolidated high schools. The tradition of neighborhood schools persisted until the 1940s, when Buck Snort's high school was consolidated with Clarksville's. By the 1950s it was apparent that neither the Cuba Landing nor the Clarksville high school could offer the programs that a countywide consolidated high school could. The state department of education therefore recommended that a consolidated high school be built in a central location. The structure would be paid for by a perpetual school tax subject to voter approval.

The combination of external pressures generated by a funding source, clear educational deficiencies, the need for a central location, and the need for voter approval of local funding presented educational decision makers with political problems. While all communities agreed that a new school was necessary, there was the problem of location. South Shiloh residents understood "central location" to refer to geography and were willing to support a tax that would endow their community with a new school. This interpretation satisfied neither the Landing nor Clarksville, however. Both would be giving up a community high school to gain better educational opportunities for their children, but neither community was willing to lose in the location decision; the tax ballot was thus in jeopardy in both Clarksville and the Landing.

The location issue was finessed by a combination of artful interpretation and word magic. Educational decision makers said that central location referred to population and not to geography, and the school was built midway between Clarksville and Cuba Landing. Once again, "they" had lied to South Shiloh.

After construction of the consolidated high school was completed, the state department of education recommended construction of a new middle school. A combination of state and local funds – earmarked for building costs alone – ensured an ability to secure bonding, but the vote was split as two board of education members held out for a newer consolidated high school and conversion of the existing building into a middle school. A forced vote would have led to a three-to-two split vote and the specter of permanent factions among board members. The decision was delayed until new board members and a new superintendent agreed to build another high school.

Financial constraints also hobbled the school system prior to industrialization in the late 1950s. Board employees refrained from cashing personal paychecks for fear that they would drive the system into insolvency. According to older board members, the 1960s continued to offer hard times: until state foundation checks arrived, Roy Martin, then the superintendent of schools, used bank loans to meet current operating expenses. When a board member suggested that the schools be closed until income and costs balanced, Martin said, "The show must go on," because state support was based on average daily attendance.

Financial problems affected the classroom at every point. Superintendent Martin favored only those recommendations designed to cut costs. Supplies were so scarce that chalk was doled out by the piece. Teachers were told, "I don't care what you teach them. Just keep them in class and keep them quiet."

When the Landing bond issue brought a $50 million metal-processing plant into Shiloh (see Chapter Two), the influx of itinerant construction workers exacerbated the schools' financial problems: school-aged children of the construction workers swamped the schools. Classes were held in gymnasiums, on stages, and in halls. The 1969 enrollment was "up a total of 81 percent over the 1960-61 level, compared to a general population increase of 25 percent."[2]

A newspaper interview with Superintendent Martin emphasized the problems brought on by industrialization:

> Taxes are a problem in Cuba Landing. The city gave the metal plant a 25-year tax-free period as an inducement to build the plant here. And this worries Shiloh County School Supt. Roy Martin. He reports that the Cuba Landing Consolidated Elementary School is old and needs renovation. Already its enrollment has grown by 60 students as a result of the boom. Martin points out that the school district's bonding power depends on the taxes it takes in. "And with the plant paying no taxes, the additional homes being built won't take care of the additional children," he said. He estimates that a new school building will be needed in five years. Under present conditions, the $500,000 cost is too steep, he said.
>
> *Solution Not Known*
>
> His solution? "I don't know," he said. Would the schools be better off if the employees lived in an adjacent county? Martin avoids this solution. He said the school system would try to gradually add classrooms, buy land for a new building, and hope for the best.[3]

The financial problems grew worse. The Shiloh County Fiscal Court issued $150 million worth of municipal industrial bonds to construct another industrial complex (see Chapter Two). The construction of this and several other facilities further increased school enrollment. The plight of the schools presented Shiloh's board of education with a problem that could not be ignored; a decision to pursue a course of developmental change was imperative.

THE BEGINNINGS

Educational change in Shiloh began with passage of a state law granting school districts the power to levy two different sets of taxes, one of which would increase real estate tax rates. The board asked the Shiloh County Fiscal Court for permission to levy this tax, and the court agreed, since it was legally bound to honor the board's request. The board then asked the court for permission to levy a 3-percent utilities use tax, and again the court's decision seemed a foregone conclusion.

But the utilities use tax met with powerful opposition. Industrial spokesmen opposed the tax because their firms would furnish the majority of the revenue. Furthermore, some factories had in-lieu-of-taxes agreements with the board, and the additional imposition of a utilities use tax would be an act of bad faith with dubious legal justification. Finally, influential community residents received long-distance telephone calls from a powerful state politician who urged opposition to the tax because it would endanger future industrial expansion in Shiloh. The calls did little, however, to dissuade them from supporting the tax.

The tension between local educational and extralocal industrial interests did produce one memorable confrontation. In a public meeting to discuss school problems, an industrial spokesman said that the citizens of Shiloh did not know what they wanted in their schools, nor what was needed, nor how to achieve either. He suggested that industry hire an independent research firm to study the county's educational system and make recommendations for improvement. The study was commissioned, but before it became public the fiscal court granted the board of education the right to tax utility use. The court's enabling action prompted industry to initiate two lawsuits: one claimed that imposition of a utilities tax voided the in-lieu-of-taxes agreement between industry and the board of education; the other argued that the board of education did not have the right to use utilities tax money to build new facilities. Industry lost both lawsuits, and the school system now had the funding to promote developmental change.

The school survey commissioned by industry was published and distributed in April 1970. The survey found no strengths in the system and made several recommendations for improvement. The system should set a new goal of improving its accreditation rank, which would require that the board of education and its administration assume a more active and innovative role in improving the schools. In particular, federal money should be sought, academic programs upgraded, and a more flexible organizational structure established. An improved accreditation rating would require building changes, including modernization, consolidation, fireproofing, and the purchase of mobile units to handle temporary classroom overflows. Recommendations were also made concerning the instructional staff, including establishing stricter standards for teaching credentials, adjusting salary schedules to make them competitive, using lay volunteers in the classes, and reducing the pupil-teacher ratio. The "most important suggestion" involved the participation of community members in defining future objectives of the school system.

Shiloh's communities reacted negatively to the survey. Buck Snort rejected the recommendation for consolidation and formed a parent-teacher association to lobby both for continued operation of the Buck Snort Elementary School and for a new school building. Cuba Landing also rejected the report: "We don't need a survey. We need money to run our schools." Clarksville objected to the recommendations on the grounds that they did not constitute a local product attuned to local needs. "They just talked to the state board and used stuff that was five years old."

At the county level the board of education, Superintendent Martin, and his assistant superintendents first viewed the report as industry's attempt to deny that educational improvement was necessary. When the report's findings made that denial untenable, an assistant superintendent said that the researchers looked for an unused tax base that would take the place of a utilities use tax. But Shiloh was taxing all sources that it legally could to support the schools, hence the recommendation that federal funds be sought.

The 1970-71 school year was an unpleasant one. The survey's findings were supported by a local teacher's testimony before a fact-finding commission concerned with state educational problems. Then teachers throughout the state held a wildcat strike that affected Shiloh's schools. Finally, Superintendent Martin suffered a fatal heart attack and the schools found themselves without executive leadership during a time of crisis. The board of education began a search for a person capable of improving the system.

The board members were in a difficult position. All but one were natives of Shiloh and thus attuned to local needs and vulnerable to local pressures. Constituents lobbied on behalf of this or that local applicant and emphasized the need for educational reform. Some suggestions focused on replacing older teachers who had inadequate credentials, yet these teachers were all native to Shiloh and had their own bases of political support. The board struck a balance between competing factions by declaring that it would seek a superintendent who could oversee a building program, which no local applicant was qualified to do.

The selection process was hampered by a dearth of qualified outside applicants; only two outside administrators with proper credentials showed interest. One was interested in the position but not in the salary offered. The other, Bill Wheeler, was willing to take a salary cut to assume this challenging responsibility. He said, "I came here because I saw the opportunity [to transform an inadequate rural educational program into] the best system in the state." Such a transformation would establish Wheeler's credentials as an educational innovator and pave the way for leadership positions in more attractive systems or perhaps even in the state department of education. For Wheeler, then, Shiloh's superintendency was a career stepping stone. Shiloh's board of education, for its part, saw Wheeler as an individual through whom it could exert strong leadership that was unaffected by communal frames of reference. Wheeler was eager for the job, he had the experience necessary to build a new system, and he had no local political bases that would make him awkward to deal with. The board therefore made Wheeler an offer, and he accepted.

The change in superintendents brought an instantaneous change in leadership style. In contrast to the slow, consensus-seeking approach to decision making, board meetings became an arena in which Wheeler recommended, the chairman called for a motion supporting the recommendation, and the motion passed unanimously.

The first set of decisions made under Wheeler's leadership reflected this new style. After looking over the school survey and accepting it as a blueprint for change, Wheeler recommended changes in building programs (remodeling the Clarksville and Landing schools and annexing a permanent addition to the existing high school to house eighth graders and thus relieve overcrowded grade schools), and in teacher-related matters (raising beginning teacher's salaries so that Shiloh's initial pay scale would be competitive with that of neighboring systems). The board approved but gave the credit for the plans to Wheeler. "When we found Bill, all we had to do was sit back. I don't think anybody could have done what he's done. He's really put this thing on the map," said the chairman.

Superintendent Wheeler pressured the seven elementary teachers who lacked bachelor's degrees to leave the system, and all of them did so. Thus, one of the survey's recommendations for instructional improvement was met and approved by the board. Wheeler deserved credit because, according to the board chairman, when the new superintendent took office, "Some of the older teachers thought they were running things." However, the forced retirements struck the remaining teachers as indicative of Wheeler's career advancement ambitions. "He'll roll anybody if it helps him get what he wants," said a teacher.

Then Wheeler strayed from the survey's recommendations. Rather than construct a new middle school, he asked that the board petition the state department of education for permission to build a new high school next to the existing structure, which could then be used as a middle school. The board concurred and petitioned for a new facilities survey; the request was granted.

At Wheeler's insistence, the facilities survey addressed the issues pertinent to local interests. At the county level, the survey recommended remodeling the board of education office, building a bus garage, and constructing a new high school; at the community level, the survey recommended providing cafeterias for Clarksville and the Landing and interim operation of the Buck Snort Elementary School. "It took a lot of politics to get [the Buck Snort decision]," said Wheeler.

The new high school reflected the recommendations that resulted from the independent school survey, specifically that the curriculum and instructional programs become flexible and individualized. The new school provided semiopen classrooms in the academic areas as a first step in meeting that recommendation. The building also provided a commons area that met another recommendation, that of giving children lunchroom space and the county a place to hold afterschool meetings, thus increasing the potential for community participation.

Wheeler then recommended that the high school academic departments abandon semester course offerings in favor of computer-scheduled, nine-week courses. Students would be allowed to select courses that appealed to them rather than being programmed into semester units on the basis of state requirements. The board concurred and these new "short-phase" courses were begun in the language arts program. Shiloh's instructional programs were becoming both flexible and individualized.

Thus, the entire school system was in transition. Most of the survey's recommendations on leadership style, building, instruction, and curriculum had been met. Leadership was flexible and entertained innovation. Buildings were changed to accommodate three grade groupings (one through five, six through eight, and nine through twelve) rather than two. The new building program created flexible space to complement a flexible instructional program; curriculum was individualized; the use of scheduled time was changed; and teachers' starting salaries were increased to attract certified beginning teachers to replace retiring older teachers. But implementing the rest of the survey's recommendations required additional money to purchase new equipment, train teachers in new instructional techniques, and support adjunct personnel. Shiloh did not have the funds to support these activities.

FORGING A SYSTEMIC LINKAGE: SHILOH'S EXPERIMENTAL SCHOOLS PROJECT

Federal money was available to fund the rest of the survey's recommendations. But the federal money was unusual. Under Lyndon Johnson's Great Society, the United States had initiated a series of domestic programs targeted at changing institutional and individual behaviors at local levels. But the Great Society was not as successful as had been hoped. Evaluating these programs, Schultze et al. observed:

> No one really knew what would work. It was possible to hire an engineer and say, "Build a bridge," but it was not possible to hire an educator and say, "Improve reading achievement in poverty schools," because educators did not know how.[4]

The authors concluded their evaluation by recommending that the federal government embark "on a program of social experimentation" to discover how to bring about changes in institutional and individual behaviors at local levels.[5]

The Experimental Schools program was such a social experiment. Rather than fund piecemeal change in a large number of schools, ES was designed to fund comprehensive educational change in a small number of selected sites. The program was based on the assumption that synergetic and lasting change would result from simultaneous changes in: (1) curriculum; (2) instruction and staffing; (3) community participation; (4) use of time, space, and facilities; and (5) organization, administration, and governance. The sponsoring agency planned to solicit letters of interest from a large number of schools interested in applying to the program and then select a small number of sites that showed experimental promise. The selected districts would receive grants for a one-year planning period. Following a year of successful planning, they would receive funding for a three-year implementation period, at the end of which another one-year contract would provide for agency phaseout and local continuation. The strategy, then, was to use federal money to fund locally planned programs of comprehensive educational change as a means of fostering lasting institutional and individual behavioral changes that would ultimately be funded at the local level.

In March 1972 an "Announcement of a Competition for Small Rural Schools" found its way to Superintendent Wheeler's desk. The announcement described a program that would enable selected rural school districts to fund locally designed programs of comprehensive educational change. It contained a set of questions, the answers to which would constitute a district's letter of interest. ES staff members and outside consultants would judge all letters of interest and select those with the most promise. Later, ES staff members would visit the districts being considered for final selection.

Wheeler recognized the opportunity outlined in the announcement. Federal money was available to fund the changes necessary to meet all the remaining recommendations of the independent school survey. Furthermore, attracting funds from such a large federal program would enhance his professional reputation as an educational innovator. All he had to do was to take advantage of this opportunity to forge a systemic linkage between the county school system and the federal ES program. The same process that had led to industrialization, imposition of a payroll tax, and improvement of services in Shiloh County was about to begin in its schools.

Wheeler started the application process. He first gained approval for Shiloh's participation from the state department of education. Although the announcement said all programs were to be locally designed and implemented, Wheeler approached his board with a request for $200 to hire a consultant team to write a letter of interest. The board authorized the expenditure. Then Wheeler called a general faculty meeting to discuss raising teachers' salaries and bringing in more instructional equipment. He needed federal money to do so, and the competition for small rural schools presented an opportunity to get federal money. Would the teachers support his efforts? All the teachers voted "Yes."

Wheeler chartered a small airplane, flew to a state university, and gave Drs. Williams and Jones, both educators with histories of successful grantsmanship, the ES announcement and the information that would answer Washington's questions. Drs. Williams and Jones composed Shiloh's letter of interest.

At one level, the letter of interest proposed a straightforward agreement. Shiloh promised to introduce individualized diagnostic instruction in all classrooms if ES underwrote expenditures for equipment, materials, teacher training, support services, and mechanisms for community participation. At another level, the letter masked a major miscommunication. Williams and Jones were experts in diagnostic instruction. In their view, attitudinal change precedes a change in habits: a teacher had to want changes in classroom performance before the changes could be implemented and routinized. Shiloh's teachers wanted equipment and more income, and they thought that was what the federal program would bring them; the teachers did not know their classroom behavior would be affected by the program.

Wheeler was not concerned with attitudinal change. He wanted to put equipment in the hands of classroom teachers, show them how to use it, and then force classroom change to occur. This approach to educational change made excellent sense to Wheeler. "There aren't that many good teachers, no matter what they say in college." Getting teachers to change required new equipment and resources: "You can't change without materials. To be a good teacher, you've got to be a good actor. But you can only act so long." When a teacher came to the end of the act, materials were necessary so that teachers could "manipulate that classroom environment to the nth degree." Force was also necessary, because teachers would not willingly accept the burdens associated with change. "The truth is, they're lazy," said Wheeler.

The promise to exchange diagnostic instruction for federal funding also made good sense to Wheeler because diagnostic instruction is "what any good coach does. It's what any good teacher should do. Besides, it's the 'in' phrase. It's where the money is."

Entrepreneurship fit Wheeler's view of himself: "If someone comes up with a good idea, I'm a pretty good exploiter." Wheeler's entrepreneurship was evident during the application process. To ensure that Shiloh's letter of interest received the proper attention, Wheeler approached Congressman Harb (the same congressman who had supported Judge Henry's bid for HUD funds to renovate the court house), who agreed to intervene in the site-selection process. But ES staff members rebuffed Harb. Wheeler was astonished that political agencies would treat an important politician in such a "high-handed manner." Wheeler figured that if Democratic Congressman Harb could not move an agency spawned by a Republican administration, perhaps Republican Senator Smith could. He used partisan ties to approach Senator Smith. On June 2, 1972 the director of ES wrote to Smith and thanked him "for your letter of May 19 in support of the application from the Shiloh County Schools." Wheeler said Senator Smith's timing was perfect; an ES review team had visited Shiloh in mid-May 1972 and had learned that the residents fully supported the schools' application. Endorsement from a powerful political player at this critical time was "helpful." A letter written by the ES director on June 25, 1972, told Senator Smith of Shiloh's selection. Five days later, a similar letter was written to Wheeler. Shiloh's schools had opportunistically forged a systemic linkage with an external agency to meet what were assumed to be local needs.

Shiloh's selection offered both the ES office in Washington, D.C., and Wheeler an attractive package. Washington supported a leader who was already promoting educational change in parts of his system and who needed funds to alter other parts. Wheeler joined a program that provided the funds to purchase new materials and equipment, to train staff in new instructional techniques, to fund support services, and to promote public awareness of school programs. In return for a minor investment, Washington gained a promising experimental site and Wheeler gained a federal program that would help transform his schools and give him great visibility in the state's coterie of educational leaders.

But there were several problems. First, the entire plan for Shiloh's ES project was based on the survey recommendations, yet the county had already rejected the survey as not being responsive to local priorities. Drs. Williams and Jones assumed that a change in attitude preceded changes in classroom performance. Wheeler was less concerned about this; he wanted to use outside funding to meet the recommendations of the survey.

Another problem was that the school survey suggested improved accreditation as a measure of change, but the ES program sought comprehensive educational change.

Third, both the authors of the school survey and the ES staff in Washington thought of schools as systems with interlocking components, but they identified minor, rather than major, variables. Schools in Shiloh were not independent organizations with sharply drawn social boundaries. Rather, schools reflected Shiloh's communal frames of reference; any planned change required consolidated support from Shiloh's kinship, neighborhood, religious, and community networks. While the school survey, Wheeler, and Washington paid lip service to community participation, they had no understanding of the importance of these communal frames of reference and the demands that they would make on any set of programs for achieving change.

Managing a Systemic Linkage: ES Project Plans

Decision Making. Some of these problems were apparent early in the planning process. Washington demanded changes in the organization, administration, and governance of ES districts. To meet these demands Wheeler took on the duties of project director and appointed as coordinators two teachers who had been influential in the school system for many years. Before the 1972-1973 school year began, both men asked to return to their regular duties because they were not in sympathy with either Wheeler or the federal program. Wheeler was pleased to have them return to teaching because they "had no faith in me." Their rejection of Wheeler and his federal program was an inauspicious beginning for planned educational change.

Gallaher distinguishes two strategies for introducing change: one is to seek consensus by allowing people to influence decisions; the other is to control events by planning for people rather than with them.[6] In contrast to traditional leadership in Shiloh, Wheeler chose the second strategy: "One man's got to do it," he said.

To ensure that his planning would be effectively carried out, Wheeler chose two new project coordinators who were adjunct personnel in the school system; one was a reading teacher with no previous administrative experience, the other an elementary guidance counselor. Neither had experience in planning educational change or in dealing with a federal bureaucracy, and neither was regarded as a leader in Shiloh's schools. Wheeler felt these were minor deficiencies since he would control planning and contact between his schools and the federal ES program. He selected the two staff members because he was sure they would be loyal to him.

His new project coordinators were loyal, but their loyalty tended to emphasize the difference between regular school operations and the federal project activities. The coordinators were located in the board of education building and were thus physically isolated from the teachers. Moreover, since planning did not require frequent consultations with administrators other than Wheeler, the coordinators were socially isolated from other members of the central office.

Thus the ES project existed in a physical and social vacuum from its inception; it was sustained as part of the school system only by virtue of Superintendent Wheeler's authority.

Process. Washington demanded community participation in the planning of Shiloh's ES project, and for Washington participation meant influencing decisions. Wheeler viewed community influence on decision making as a trespass on his authority and used various techniques to control participation. He and his coordinators visited various civic and fraternal organizations to acquaint their members with the new project and to ask for advice on setting priorities. The members of these organizations were delighted with Shiloh's selection as an ES site ("How'd you get so lucky?") and offered many suggestions for change. Wheeler then decided which of the suggestions were valid and should be incorporated into the local plan and which should be discarded. In effect, he was acting as a gatekeeper, placing himself between Shiloh's communities and schools, and a planned program of educational change.

A community advisory committee was formed in response to Washington's demand for community participation in the planning process. The committee made two recommendations that were incorporated into the final plan: one was establishment of a diagnostic center offering specialized adjunct services to the schools; the other was the use of appropriate measures to help Shiloh County children meet national norms on standardized achievement tests in reading and mathematics. Wheeler was in favor of including the diagnostic center in the plan; it would be located in the middle school and its staff would include a reading clinician; a nurse; a guidance counselor; and contract personnel skilled in social work, psychological counseling, and the diagnosis of speech and hearing problems. Meeting national norms on standardized achievement tests became a major project goal. In order to improve student scores, Wheeler accepted the advice of two faculty members and introduced two packaged programs in reading and mathematics, each of which used a wide variety of materials designed for individualized instruction.

Once the reading and mathematics programs were under way in the semiopen space provided by learning centers in the elementary and middle schools, Wheeler was confident that children in grades three through eight would score at national levels on standardized achievement tests. He was convinced that both programs were "teacher-proof," or impervious to teacher manipulation, and that mandatory use of new materials would bring about a change in classroom behavior. "The great damned thing about canned programs is this: they give the teachers a reference point to go from. I think we put the kid in the center of the program. Hell, that is individualizing – if you can get the teacher out of the way," said Wheeler.

The superintendent's chosen role forced him to deal with another set of actors – the Washington, D.C., staff of the ES program. This was not an easy task. With the first official notification of Shiloh's selection as an ES site, the director of ES had indicated that his staff was looking "forward to working cooperatively in the days ahead in the translation of your ideas into reality."[7] Wheeler soon discovered that this cooperation was at odds with his conception of project direction.

During August 1972 Ms. Flowers, a member of the ES staff in Washington, D.C., visited Shiloh County. Her thank-you note glowed with goodwill. "The grass is *definitely* greener in our small school sites."[8] But Wheeler had not completely controlled the course of her visit, a fact apparent in her promise to send him "a more specific scope of work that will reflect our recent discussion, as well as an outline for the first report due September 15." This letter ended a cooperative arrangement between equals and signaled the advent of an adversarial relationship between patron and client. Control of the planning process was at stake.

The adversarial relationship came into full view when the first local plan was sent to Washington, D.C., by September 15, 1972. The plan triggered stinging criticism. In a letter dated October 4 Washington said that the report raised serious questions about the planning process, particularly in four areas.[9] First, there was no coordination of effort evident; there were a host of committees, but they had no assigned tasks. This would have to be changed. Second, although Wheeler had said that the final plan would be Shiloh's, the report said that two consultants were working in Shiloh. Washington wanted to know why a visiting professor of education (Dr. Williams) had informed committee members about the problems and goals of education:

> Why should he (or any other outsider) be explaining the problems and goals of education to parents? Since the mode of communication was presentation and then question and answer, there was little chance for discussion. Most of the questions raised cannot rightfully be answered by an outside con-

> sultant. There was not one question that was answered directly, as at least one person in attendance suggested at the end of the meeting. We simply reiterate what we have said before . . . that the best experts on Shiloh are in Shiloh and they are the ones best qualified to determine what help is needed.

The letter also questioned Wheeler's approach to community participation:

> When and how does the public get to *influence* the status of the project? It is absolutely vital to the success of the project that there be substantive, two-way communication with community about the plans. Community should have the chance to be in on the planning, not just to hear about it after the fact.

Finally, the letter questioned whether any meaningful documentation was taking place.

Wheeler's reaction to ES staff queries was one of instantaneous compliance; he feared that failure to do as Washington wished would lead to contract cancellation. When the letter was received, Dr. Williams was escorted to the local airport and put aboard a plane. His perception of the event was that he had been fired.

The letter had a number of consequences for planning. Wheeler would not be able to rely on the expertise of a consultant to pull the diverse elements of the plan into a coherent document. Furthermore, Wheeler's role as gatekeeper ended. Instead he became a "living link" or liaison among all the social systems engaged in the systemic linkage. Wheeler had to coordinate the exchanges among Shiloh's communal frames of reference, Shiloh's schools, the piecemeal contributions of various consultants, and the ES staff in Washington, D.C. The living link role fragmented Wheeler's performance, and this fragmentation was reflected in the emerging plan. When Dr. Williams next saw the federal project plan, he called it a "plotless novel," a product of disjointed thinking.

The lack of consultant help affected Wheeler in another way. He saw part of his role as that of salesman who needed an expert to convince his local audiences of the merits of his plan. But Washington would not allow the use of consultants, so Wheeler had to allow community members to influence planning and then demonstrate that influence to Washington. The incorporation of a diagnostic center and the attainment of national norms on standardized achievement tests did this.

The planning period was rife with confrontations between Washington and Wheeler. The December 15, 1972, report to Washington attempted to respond to the criticisms spelled out in the October 4 letter. The process of producing the report overwhelmed Shiloh's board of education staff, and the final version was not completed until the early morning of December 15. A project coordinator caught an airplane and hand-carried the document to the ES offices in Washington. This effort elicited another critical response, dated January 24, 1973.[10] The letter said that the December 15 submission was an interim document to be corrected by February 15, 1973. The major criticisms were that the plan's central theme and goals were "vague and general statements about the realities of education and life . . . . The plan, at present, is a collection of loose ideas, not an integrated, tightly woven plan." Community involvement was still a problem:

> Although the theme states the great importance of community involvement and community-wide effort, the section on community is one of the weakest. There is contradiction between statements made in the section on administration and governance about decision making and those in the section on community.

All of these weaknesses would have to be corrected.

The February 15 submission was no more successful. During her visit to Shiloh in March 1972, Ms. Flowers made no mention of the latest submission until twenty minutes before her departure, at which point she loosed a barrage of criticism and then left before she could be asked for advice on corrections. A project coordinator complained, "Had we been funded, I would have told her what I thought of her. As it was, I kept my mouth shut." The structure of systemic linkages, which put the purse in Washington's hands and the supplicant's bowl in Shiloh's, precluded action on Shiloh's part.

In response to Washington's demand for early implementation, Wheeler arranged for Drs. Frankel and Ribbon, two university consultants with expertise in behavior modification, to instruct his faculty. Unfortunately, they needed videotapes of actual classroom performance to do this, and Washington had not yet approved the purchase of the videotape machines. Therefore, the teachers were given a standard lecture rather than a demonstration of the techniques of behavior modification. They rejected the program, which in turn prompted Wheeler to express his displeasure with the consultants.

While Wheeler struggled for control of the systemic linkage, he kept knowledge of the conflict from the rest of the county, and the public was delighted with the changes in the schools. "Our Schools . . . They're On Their Way" ran a November front-page headline in the *Shiloh Crier.* The article noted that all of the school survey's recommendations were being met save one – community participation. Wheeler was quoted as saying "This is the hardest area to implement. We attempt to do this utilizing the *Shiloh Crier* . . . the radio, and parent groups and teacher news letters and still we fall short."

Thus, despite Washington's best efforts to assure community participation in planning, Wheeler merely followed the independent school survey's recommendation to inform Shiloh's communities about planned changes; he did not allow them to influence planning. Wheeler explained his position by saying that community influence on decision making was nonessential at best. "Let's be realistic. People judge a school on how the football and basketball teams do, how the band marches, and on how their kids feel when they come home." Washington did not understand this, and their demands hurt his cause because they acted like "kids playing games. They're theorizing. I'm implementing. There's a big difference."

The project coordinators loyally supported Wheeler's view of the ES staff in Washington, D.C.: the criticisms of their submissions created "impossible demands" and Washington provided no constructive help. "They were always in conference when we called them."

Toward the end of the planning year, a regional visitation team visited the Shiloh County schools. One of the visitors, a personal friend of Wheeler, was shown through the partially completed school.

The friend had thought of entering his district in the ES competition but had decided not to because he figured participation in the program would be too much trouble. Wheeler said that given younger teachers, a new set of materials for classrooms, and the chance to train the teaching staff in the use of new technologies, it would be possible to implement a flexible, individualized instructional program. "Age doesn't have a damn thing to do with teaching." said his friend. Wheeler disagreed. "I can bullshit the younger ones," he claimed.

The final episode in the planning process came after the beginning of implementation. Once again Ms. Flowers visited Shiloh. This time she voiced no dissatisfaction with the plan. Instead, she conveyed a message about time: Shiloh County had a year and a half to implement what it had planned and no more. The timetable was crucial; in Washington's negotiations with all rural sites for further funding, only success would be rewarded.

The Final Plan. As a "blueprint" (as Wheeler called it) for educational change in the classroom, the 100-page final ES plan reflected the goal of the federal project to use materials, equipment, teacher training, and consultant expertise to establish individualized diagnostic instruction in every classroom. This goal was set by Drs. Williams and Jones because their research showed that the dominant mode of teaching in the state was group instruction, which was inadequate because it ignored individual variation. The opening statement of the problem in Shiloh's ES plan evidenced their dissatisfaction with such a model:

> The current educational program in Shiloh County is characterized by sameness – the same experiences, the same textbooks, and for most students, the same assignments and the same resultant boredom. In other words, a child's educational experience has been textbook centered. Little regard, if any, has been given to the child's individual needs, interests, and abilities.[11]

The federal project would change this model by inserting both packaged and teacher-made materials into the curricula and by showing teachers how to use diagnostic instruction to individualize classroom teaching.

From another perspective, the plan reflected a fusion process at the planning (or executive) level of Shiloh's school administration. The independent school survey recommended changes in accreditation, leadership style, building, support services, curricula and instruction, and community participation. Washington demanded changes in curricula, instruction and staffing; community participation; use of time, space, and facilities; and organization, administration, and governance. Wheeler fused the two agendas for change. He introduced a building program to change the use of space and facilities. The switch from semester classes to short-phased courses altered the system's use of time. To ensure community participation as recommended by the school survey, Wheeler flooded the news media with positive accounts of his schools and supported extracurricular activities, such as football, basketball, and band, that gave the schools local prominence. Wheeler had initiated staffing changes before the ES project began by recruiting young teachers with professional credentials. Later he used federal funds to create a support service – the diagnostic center – and to alter both curricula and instructional techniques. The only recommendation left unmet was that of improved accreditation, but the new buildings, curricula, instructional techniques, and support services would ensure its satisfaction.

Shiloh's first quarterly report to Washington began with a statement reflecting this second perspective:

> In order to comprehend the changes that have transpired within the Shiloh County School System . . . one must first look at the needs as pointed out . . . by a professional, independent survey team. The Experimental Schools Project did allow for planning and a means to provide for joint utilization of local, state, and federal funds. It has become increasingly difficult to separate the Experimental Schools Project from the rest of the system.[12]

The fusion of federal and local agendas also met the county's goal of promoting developmental changes that would attract new residents. The ES plan included a fictionalized case study as an illustration of how developmental change in the schools was expected to help attract outsiders to the county:

> The Crawfords, a family of five with three school age children, moved to Shiloh from California so that Mr. Crawford could take a position as an industrial engineer. The contrast between urban and rural America put the Crawfords into culture shock.
>
> Then Mrs. Crawford got a job as a teacher. She found the programs offered by the Shiloh County Schools were superior to those in California. Her children not only received individualized instruction, they were also given expert diagnostic service and guidance from specialized personnel in the diagnostic center.
>
> All the Crawfords were pleased with the schools after a year's time. Mr. Crawford said that "the curriculum emphasizes many approaches that his former place of residence is considering developing in a model school." The Crawfords "feel that Shiloh County is an excellent place for children to develop in their own style and at their own rate."[13]

From a third perspective, the plan was a naive political document, based on the assumption that a systemic linkage, with Wheeler acting as a living link, could be imposed on Shiloh's schools to alter traditional classroom behavior. Shiloh's teachers had agreed to enter the program because they would receive money for participating and because the program would bring new materials into their classrooms. When the teachers discovered that Washington expected fundamental changes in individual and institutional behavior, their response was predictable, strong, and effective. Wheeler was not native to the county and had minimal access to its political processes. About 50 percent of the teachers were natives, and a majority of the remaining 50 percent had married county residents and thus were familiar with Shiloh's communal frames of reference and the political processes that could intervene in a systemic linkage. When it became clear that the teachers were using these processes to change the course of the project, Dr. Williams said, "I don't know of a superintendent in the state who could pull this off."

But there was one who would try. Wheeler's professional reputation depended on transforming Shiloh's schools, and he did not intend to let the teachers frustrate his efforts. His style of leadership was summarized by a project coordinator: "What you [have to] do is provide the time, the money, and the threat."

The teachers could not avoid the federal project by going to another school system because the supply of teachers far exceeded demand in the 1970s, and Shiloh's teachers knew this. With no hope of relocation, their only alternatives were to change their traditional classroom performance or use Shiloh's communal frames of reference to generate sufficient political power to counter Wheeler's efforts. The succeeding chapters tell what happened, how, and why.

Notes

1. U.S. Congress, Public Law 92-318 (Washington, D.C.: Government Printing Office, 1972), p. 390.
2. *A Survey of the School System of Shiloh County* (St. Louis, Mo.: ABC Research, 1970), p. 18.
3. *Survey of the School System*, pp. 165-166.
4. Schultze et al., *Setting National Priorities*, p. 452.
5. Ibid., p. 463.

6. Art Gallaher Jr., "Directed Change in Formal Organizations", in *Change Processes in the Public Schools* (Eugene, Oregon: Center for the Advanced Study of Educational Administration, University of Oregon, 1965), p. 41.
7. National Institute of Education, Experimental Schools program, Letter to Shiloh County Board of Education, dated June 30, 1972.
8. Ibid., Aug. 31, 1972.
9. Ibid., Oct. 4, 1972.
10. Ibid., Jan. 24, 1973.
11. Shiloh County Board of Education, "Shiloh County Experimental Schools Plan," 1973, typed manuscript, p. 1.
12. Shiloh County Board of Education, "Quarterly Report No. 1 to Experimental Schools," October 1973, typed manuscript, p. 1.
13. "Shiloh County Experimental Schools Plan," p. 100.

4

Administrative Behavior: Imposing Developmental Change on Shiloh's Schools

The conflict between Wheeler and his teachers was not a problem unique to Shiloh; similar problems beset other programs in which national policy directives were imposed upon local units attempting to achieve developmental change. The critical factor in using systemic linkages to bring about change is the skill of local living links: "The payoff to the program depends more on the insights and competence of managers on the scene than on the wisdom of those directing the program in Washington."[1] The relevant question, then, is whether Wheeler's style of leadership, which focused on planning for people rather than with them, was capable of overcoming resistance. This chapter describes Wheeler's leadership during program implementation, beginning with the August 1973 in-service workshop designed to introduce the federal plan to Shiloh's teachers and ending with the board of education's apparent offer of a new four-year contract for Wheeler beginning in January 1975.

The Experimental Schools program required changes in organization, administration, and governance. Wheeler met those requirements by assuming the duties of project director and by appointing two project coordinators. Neither coordinator had been influential in the school system before assuming these new duties, and neither maintained systematic contact with teachers or administrators during the planning phase. The coordinators were influential in the schools only because they were backed by Wheeler's authority as superintendent.

The official duties of the coordinators during the implementation phase furthered the social and physical distance between them and the regular teaching staff. For example, the project plan stated that all teachers would attend the in-service workshops. A project coordinator was responsible for keeping attendance records. The coordinator's power to force teachers to do something out of the ordinary underlined the social distance between project staff and teachers. This distance was symbolized during the in-service workshop by the coordinators' choice of seating. The attendance sheet was placed on a table overlooking the commons area of the partially completed high school. Teachers had to go to the table and write their names on the roster. The two coordinators sat at the table while signatures were matched with physical presence, and they remained there during the subsequent in-service training session. As an elementary school teacher later remarked, "You wonder if it [the ES project] ever got going. It got started with people resenting things. Like taking attendance at in-service."

Wheeler widened the social distance between project and regular staff with his opening address to the faculty. He said that the plan contained a major flaw. "The weakness of this project here is that there has not been enough teacher input." But Wheeler's style of leadership would compensate for the lack of input. The teachers had to read the federal plan: "This is a blueprint and this is going to be the way we operate the schools. Now is the time to start pulling things together."

The teachers felt that the plan violated their authority in the classroom by demanding individualized instruction, which they saw as allowing students to do as they pleased. The project was not congruent with Shiloh's traditional concept of proper classroom teaching nor with the way the rest of society operated. An elementary teacher voiced opposition, saying, "That's my biggest beef. You can't let a child do as he wants. When you get a job, you can't do what you want. You do what you have to." A high school teacher agreed: "Nobody gets to do their thing outside." Another high school teacher added, ["With individualized instruction] I'm afraid we'll lose the kids."

Two high school teachers expressed the faculty's perspective on the federal program, project staff, and Superintendent Wheeler. One criticized the planning process that produced the plan and said, "I'd like to see it programmed by a teacher, not a flop that's moved up." Another complained about Wheeler's leadership style: "When he first came here, you could talk to him. But he doesn't want to do that anymore."

Wheeler's presentation to the faculty focused on deficiencies in the instructional program. He noted that Shiloh's reading achievement test scores were at national levels up through the fourth grade. From that point the scores dropped at an accelerating rate. The federal project had funded the purchase of new reading and mathematics programs which supplied the materials and direction necessary to meet national norms in grades three through eight. In the new high school an individualized, basic mathematics course would help correct deficiencies. The new programs would make Shiloh County a leader in southern education. "There's not a lot of southern systems that will place 50 percent of its students above national norms. As a matter of fact, I don't know of any," said Wheeler.

Aggressiveness was a dominant theme in Wheeler's approach to educational change. "I've been told fifty times that it can't be done, and I've agreed with them. But we will do it." Wheeler had good reason to be determined: "When I first came here, I told them I'd give them the best system in the state in four years. When we got the federal money, I dropped it to three. This is my third year."

A great deal would be demanded of the teachers. "There is going to be a tremendous amount of pressure on each and every one of you. We are trying to accomplish in three years what should take eight," said Wheeler. But some teachers were not impressed. "You learn to live with pressure. It doesn't bother me," said a secondary school teacher. An elementary school teacher echoed this sentiment when she later observed that the pressure at the in-service workshops slackened after classes started.

The attitudinal split between Wheeler and his teaching staff was sharpened by a series of confrontations during the fall of 1973. Aware that the faculty was unhappy with his demands for change, Wheeler met with teachers in every school. At the middle school he asked for and won a vote of confidence in his leadership. But in the new high school teachers were less tractable. Wheeler told the high school teachers that they were not treating his new building with the care it deserved; litter on the floor and disordered books shelves proved this. Teachers blamed poor janitorial service for the litter. One influential teacher who had left the project coordinator position to return to the high school said that untidy bookshelves were cause for praise, not censure, because they indicated that students used the books. Wheeler left the meeting, kicking a wastepaper basket as he went. "If you don't like the way I'm running things, go to the board," he said in parting.

Approached by several teachers, members of the board of education claimed that Wheeler was a "go-getter" who was transforming

Shiloh's schools. The teachers were unable to build a political constituency that would curb Wheeler's style of leadership. But they at least convinced the board to recommend that Wheeler take a vacation; the teachers were afraid that he would "go berserk" if he did not get some rest. Wheeler refused, arguing that the changes he was introducing required his constant supervision.

Wheeler's perception of the high school confrontation was different from the teachers' views. He complained that by publicly contradicting him, influential teachers were undermining his authority, and he would not allow it. "I'm accountable and so are they . . . . I've been bragging them up for two years, telling everyone how young they are. The truth is they're sloppy and lazy. They don't use their students to clean up their rooms or line their chairs up." Strong leadership would change this.

Wheeler's janitorial foray had two consequences. One was intentional: his demands for better housekeeping led teachers to use students as janitors. Two blackboard messages in the new high school celebrated their new cleanliness:

This Room Is
Germ-Proof
Anti-Bacterial
Disinfected
And
Clean

This Room Is Germ-Proof,
Anti-Bacterial, Disinfected
And
Cleaner Than
Mr. Morgan's Room

The second consequence was unintended. By the time the janitorial battle had been fought and won, teachers had gained the support of one board member, who complained to Wheeler that he was usurping board power, and there were community complaints on other matters. The board member's complaints had no effect. Wheeler ignored the criticism, noting that even though board support for him was not unanimous, it was split four to one in his favor. The teachers continued to complain to the dissident board member, but they did not yet have the support to curb Wheeler officially.

The teachers' lack of board support was apparent in the spring of 1974, when the Shiloh County Educational Association circulated a questionnaire among all teachers to help define teacher-administrator conflicts. All respondents agreed that there was a "communications gap" between the faculty and Wheeler. These findings were discussed in a teachers' meeting, at which Wheeler took the floor and admitted that the communications gap was real and had to be solved. He proceeded to widen the gap as he spoke about the problem of personal leave.

A teacher had asked for one day of personal leave to attend to business in a city ninety miles distant. Wheeler had refused to allow her a day's leave. He justified his decision with an example: "Let's say that fifty people wanted to take a personal day to work in an election. What would I do?"

"Hire fifty substitutes," said a teacher. Wheeler would not do this, a position that prompted the president of the association to urge teachers to attend the next meeting of the board of education. The meeting was to be a test of strength – the teachers pitted against Wheeler, with the board as umpire.

The association came before the next meeting of the board, and the chairman recognized the delegation, saying, "What're you getting ready to do? Throw a fit, or what?" The president of the association presented a list of grievances. In particular, the president argued for a teacher's right to use personal days without Wheeler's prior approval. She based her argument on the idea of professionalism: "Teachers are a professional group. You're trusting us with the most valuable asset in the county, the children," she said. Professionalism ensured that the teachers' use of personal days would not be detrimental to the system.

Although the teachers obviously had minimal support for their cause at this point, the president of the association pressed for a resolution. "We were hoping for some board action tonight," she said.

"No. We have to give Bill time," said a board member.

The delegation left the meeting and later said their efforts had been wasted; they had no support. Wheeler controlled the schools.

But Wheeler's control was showing the first signs of slippage. The board's support seemed to be wavering, especially when one board member asked Wheeler what the problem was because, "They've already got what they're asking for."

Wheeler was silent. The teachers really did not have what they were asking for, despite board policy to the contrary. Although the board had consented to allow teachers to take personal days off without prior approval, Wheeler had refused to allow one elementary teacher to do so. His refusal to go along with board policy led to the delegation's demand. Recognizing that the delegation betokened rebellion in the schools, the chairman of the board warned, "This thing is getting out of hand."

Indeed, some teachers had support from various groups that represented Shiloh's communal frames of reference, and this led to a significant straw vote at the next board meeting. Several teachers, including the band director, were up for tenure. Wheeler said that the Band Boosters were demanding additional money for the band, based on the contention that the band was the one school-based unit with a record of great success. It had won several first prizes in marching competitions against well-known regional bands, one of which had played in the Olympic Games. Wheeler claimed that this demand was sparked by the band director's complaints and was a deliberate attempt to undermine Wheeler's authority by appealing to an external organization.

Wheeler wanted to fire the band director. His request put the board in a difficult situation. The Band Boosters were a county-wide organization which represented every major communal and political group. Firing the band director would be dangerous, "[He's] doing a wonderful job," said the chairman.

"That's saying 'back up.' I don't want to spend the whole next year being a villain to the Band Boosters," said Wheeler.

The meeting turned to a discussion of the teachers eligible for tenure. "Is there anything we ought to talk about before we put them on tenure? Once they're on tenure, they're there. Are there any that you can't get along with?" asked a board member.

"Can I clear the room?" asked Wheeler. The board voted to go into executive session. When the spectators had left, Wheeler said, "I realize that at this time it would create a tremendous amount of controversy, and most of you would be on the side of the band director. I've had my mind made up all day to fire him."

"I don't think he himself is trying to rig this thing," said a board member who had kinsmen in the band.

"If we can't control him, then we're in trouble," said another, also with several kinsmen in the band. This latter board member's constituents also organized activities such as community cookouts, to raise money for the band.

Wheeler pressed for dismissal.

"I couldn't vote against him," said a board member. The chairman agreed, and his decision was significant because he had the power to recognize or not recognize any motion made by a board member.

"If it comes up that Bill can't work with him, then our hands are tied," argued a board member who had no relatives in the band.

Wheeler said that at issue was the use of an organization external to the schools to undermine his authority, not whether this or that teacher gained tenure. "I had the same trouble [with a coach]. It's not professional conduct."

A board member with relatives in the band asked the board's attorney for an opinion. The attorney said that insubordination was cause for dismissal, regardless of tenure, so the board had an acceptable alternative: "If he keeps stirring, and we can prove it, that's it."

The chairman remarked that the issue was being blown out of proportion; the board had sufficient power to deal with such problems. "If we can't handle him, the boy he is, then we're pretty weak."

"Hell. We are weak," claimed another board member who was mindful of the strength of Shiloh's communal frames of reference in political decision making.

Wheeler lost the battle; the board gave the band director tenure. News of the events in the closed meeting spread through the county as board members discussed the matter with their relatives, neighbors, and friends, who confirmed the wisdom of the board's decision to grant tenure. The decision was further validated by the number of favorable telephone calls each board member received from constituents. But the issue brought school conflicts out in the open, and public sentiment was turning against Wheeler. "There's been a lot of talk about firing Bill," said a member of the Band Boosters immediately after the tenure decision.

Teachers tried to further public dissatisfaction during the summer of 1974. They visited friends, neighbors, and relatives with tales of Wheeler's actions. One teacher recalled such a visit to the chairman of the board. The chairman was upset because Wheeler's behavior was drawing public comment and putting pressure on him. "We've got to live here after Bill's gone," said the chairman, who then confided, "We're looking hard at Trane [an assistant superintendent, as a possible replacement]."

"Don't look at Trane. Look at Collins," said the teacher. This advice carried weight since the teacher had been employed in the school system for many years; had extensive community ties based on marriage, residence, and long service in various community and fraternal organizations; and was a neighbor of the chairman. Moreover, Collins was also native to the county, had extensive familial ties, had lived in all three of Shiloh's communities, and had served in the schools as guidance counselor, teacher, and principal for twenty years.

The issue of succession was brought to a head by Wheeler himself. During a summer board meeting in 1974, he said that the coming year was the last in his contract and that he would not ask for reappointment. When pressed by the board for his reasons, he said that the changes started by his federal project would require a "bull to keep them going," and he was tired.

"We'll do everything we can to change your mind," said a board member. The chairman thought Wheeler's decision was understandable. "We're not paying you near enough." A third board member scoffed at the superintendent's decision. "He wants us to beg him to come back." However, Wheeler offered another reason for not returning: "You can't use people the way I do without it catching up," he said.

The teachers' campaign against Wheeler entered a new phase in the 1974-75 school year. Instead of relying solely on political pressure to change his behavior, they also resorted to social shunning (see Chapter Six). Just as the habit of cursing led to a member of the Baptist church being "churched" (see Chapter One), Wheeler's style of leadership led to his social isolation.

At a two-week in-service workshop preceding the 1974-75 school year, Wheeler again addressed the faculty about the demands of change. "I assure you that we are in for a brutal year," he said. The burdens of change would affect the high school in particular. "The high school has a lot to do. You have to get ready for the Southern Association evaluation." The evaluation would be conducted by an accreditation team from the Southern Association of Colleges and Schools. Membership in the association would give the high school the highest accreditation in the region and would meet the goal recommended by the independent school survey. Membership would also validate Wheeler's leadership, for if the high school were admitted to the association, Wheeler could take credit for having transformed an inadequate rural system into a school system that was competitive with the best in the region.

The decision to join the Southern Association also signaled Wheeler's recognition of the fact that his federal project was in trouble. Rather than striving to attain the prestige that successful implementation of diagnostic instruction would bring, Wheeler wanted to use the evidence of new buildings, curricula, equipment, and the prestige of having been chosen to participate in the federal project to improve the accreditation rating and thereby add lustre to his credentials in preparation for moving to another position. "He's doing what he's been doing since he got here. He's getting ready for his next job," said the popular high school teacher who had left the project coordinator's position.

During Wheeler's presentation at the 1974-75 in-service workshop, the teachers were united in their opposition to him for the first time. They were like students required to listen to an unpopular lecture: they scrutinized the ceiling, inspected the floor, exchanged glances with their neighbors, fiddled with pencils and papers, and passed notes. One teacher later remarked, "Did you see their faces? They're not listening anymore."

Wheeler had seen their faces and had drawn his own conclusions. Later in the day he discussed what had happened to his plans for creating a "first-class school system" in Shiloh. His ambition for change had dwindled along with his authority to enforce change. He no longer had the power to compel the teachers to obey him. "I'm whipped. And I don't whip easily," he admitted.

But he was not totally whipped, as subsequent events demonstrated. Several teachers claimed that other duties took precedence over the in-service workshop and did not attend. Wheeler told the principals that attendance was required and that refusal to attend would constitute insubordination and cause for immediate dismissal. This information was relayed to the teachers not attending, who rearranged their schedules to attend the workshop. Not satisfied with their compliance, Wheeler told Collins, the high school principal, that the teachers' absence was evidence of incompetent leadership. Incompetence would lead to reassignment.

When news of Wheeler's threat spread through the school, the faculty gave Collins a public vote of confidence and set aside the next day's noon hour for a luncheon in his honor. They also complained to a board member about Wheeler's threat, and the board member promised that no one would be fired or reassigned. Word of his backing quickly spread among the teachers; this was their first public success in curbing Wheeler.

However, Wheeler still enjoyed considerable authority. The accreditation team spent three days in the high school and found only minor deficiencies. Wheeler immediately corrected the problems, and the high school was admitted to the association. The goal of improved accreditation had been met, and Wheeler had public confirmation that his leadership had transformed Shiloh's schools.

But there was no such confirmation that his leadership had met the goals of the federal project. Mr. Season, Ms. Flowers's successor at the ES office in Washington, D.C., was in Shiloh during the accreditation team's visit. He said that membership in the association was a "capstone" but that the success of the schools did not equal the success of the federal project. Voicing his concerns to Wheeler had little effect, however, because neither Wheeler nor the ES office in Washington had the power to go beyond the social boundaries of the systemic linkage to enforce unwanted change on Shiloh's schools.

One of the reasons why Shiloh's schools had moved beyond the boundaries of the typical systemic linkage was the recent course of events in Washington. The National Institute of Education was under severe congressional criticism, one result of which was a decreased budget. Lack of funds forced the agency to examine the value of all its programs. Mr. Season told the Shiloh County Board of Education, "In order to ensure the continued funding of Project Rural, we may need some help." Specifically, Mr. Season wanted to use Shiloh as a demonstration site so that other agency staff could visit a school system that had been successful in implementing comprehensive educational change. Shiloh County was reported to have the most successful program that ES was funding. "You've come a long way in a short period of time. There's no doubt about that," said Mr. Season.

Wheeler agreed to this proposal. Later he assessed Mr. Season's request from a local political perspective. During the application process, the planning year, and the first year of program implementation, Washington had had the power to dictate policy to Shiloh's schools. Now the positions of power in the systemic linkage were reversed: Washington was the supplicant, and Shiloh was the almsgiver. "They're really begging, aren't they?" said Wheeler.

Wheeler described the shift in power to the board after Mr. Season had departed. "I wish we were starting again because we'd get three times as much money," he said. But since Wheeler could not turn back the clock, he would be content with a new relationship with Washington. "I've reached the point . . . where I'm going to get a little aggressive. I'm really not going to take any more from these people in Washington. . . . I've beat them." Wheeler had seized control of the systemic linkage between Shiloh's schools and Washington. The major limitation was that he was in the process of losing his own local power base.

The validation of change went beyond improved accreditation and an altered relationship with Washington. Wheeler arranged for a television crew from the state department of education to film the schools and to show the film on educational television. The board consented to this arrangement provided that the teachers had no objection.

Wheeler set about to ensure that the teachers would comply with his wishes. He first taped a speech on the topic of opening the schools to public scrutiny. He then called a meeting with the middle school faculty. On his way from the board of education to the middle school, Wheeler said of his speech, "Most of this is bullshit." Asked if the speech would move his teachers to decide to allow the filming, he said, "Hell. [The decision has] already been made."

Wheeler told his middle school faculty the purpose of the meeting and then played the taped speech. At the end of the recording he said, "If the total faculty agrees to open it up, it'll be opened. If not, no." He asked each faculty member if he or she had any objection to filming the schools. One faculty member did, but Wheeler prevailed. The teacher finally said, "Open it up, of course. I don't mind them coming. I don't care."

"They wanted to say 'no.' That's what I call positive leadership," said Wheeler later.

He reported his findings to the board:

> I was asked to check with the teachers and see if that was what they wanted. I tried to put it to them bluntly. It's a big ball game. Basically the teachers want this. There's not a doubt in my mind. I'm not in this for any glory for myself. I've got the glory. I've got the connections. My reputation was established when I got an $880,000 grant. They're still scratching their heads on how I got that. What do you all think about this TV program? You told me to do it and I did. Now, what do you think?

"If the teachers want it . . . " started a board member.

"It's not the teachers' decision," interrupted Wheeler. The board voted to allow the filming of the schools.

The filming provoked an incident symbolic of the entire process of change in Shiloh's schools. A teacher had assigned several students to perform for the camera but was reluctant to go before the camera herself. Wheeler asked the teacher to do so several times, but the teacher refused. The superintendent took hold of her arm and shoved her before the camera. "Get your tail in there," he said.

After being filmed the teacher, in tears, said, "I've never had anyone talk to me like that before." Another teacher said that the members of the board of education would hear of the incident. "They're going to be barraged with calls tonight," she said. The calls would affect the chairman of the board in particular. The reluctant camera performer was the daughter of the teacher who had led her elementary classes outside the Landing's consolidated elementary school during the heat of spring and fall despite her principal's threats to those who left the building. The neighboring and kinship ties that had led to the principal's dismissal were still active, although slightly altered – the teacher's kinsman who had been a member of the board was now chairman of it.

By this time, there was an informal alliance among teachers, some community residents, several court house politicians, and two board members. All wanted Wheeler to make the decision to leave Shiloh, but as Wheeler said, he did not have any place to go. Therefore, he counted on the support of residents who continued to favor educational change and on the backing of three board members, since two board votes were not enough to oust him. A teacher who was opposed to Wheeler analyzed the political situation and concluded that the teachers would lose in a board vote. "You need three. I mean one's got to be a cousin. You got to catch one stealing. You need three. You can't have any wobblers."

The board meeting of January 9, 1975, showed that Wheeler indeed had three supporting votes. He told the board that a number of other superintendents in the state had been fired and then asked, "What's your pleasure?"

"When do we do this? In April?" asked a board member who wanted more time to consolidate opposition to Wheeler.

"You're going to do it right now," said Wheeler.

One board member made a motion that Wheeler be given a new four-year contract. The motion was seconded and carried, four to one. It looked as though Wheeler's style of leadership, which focused on planning for people rather than with them, was not totally ineffective or inappropriate. Although unable to force teachers to implement his plan for comprehensive educational change, he was able to transform Shiloh's schools; to draw favorable national, regional, state, and local attention to his programs of change; and to retain his position as superintendent. Consolidated opposition based upon Shiloh's communal frames of reference appeared to be unequal to the task of challenging Wheeler's leadership.

Notes

1. Schultze et al., *Setting National Priorities*, p. 453.

5

Barriers to Imposed Developmental Change: Shiloh's Teachers and Students

As a result of Wheeler's leadership, the schools now had the credentials to confirm their transformation, which should have met with teacher approval. Instead, the teachers were trying to oust Wheeler from the system. The reasons for their resistance can be examined from two perspectives.

The larger perspective concerns a problem that typically plagues federal programs in which national policy is implemented in the form of changes imposed on small local units. In his analysis of Lyndon Johnson's Great Society programs, Charles Schultze et al. first focused on a particular federal assumption: "The idea persisted that if one could identify a problem and allocate some federal money to it, the problem would get solved."[1] The assumption proved false. By seeking "to change fundamental behavior patterns of individuals and institutions,"[2] many of the new programs invited local resistance. This was precisely the situation in Shiloh County. Wheeler was demanding that the teachers replace traditional teaching roles with newer models. The teachers were not willing to do this, and student response supported their resistance.

The narrower perspective focuses on instructional styles and curricula. The teachers in Shiloh were used to the lecture model of instruction, which they had learned in school, church, and other community organizations. The traditional teaching model consisted of (1) assignment of a textbook unit to the class; (2) lecture/discussion based on the text; (3) group testing on the unit; and (4) guidance through the next unit in the textbook. The new model demanded teacher: (1) determination of school purposes; (2) diagnosis of each student's needs and learning characteristics; (3) development of a curriculum congruent with these needs and characteristics; and (4) presentation of the curriculum using various modes of instruction to meet the needs of individual students in the classroom.

Diagnostic instruction not only required replacement of well-established teaching models, it also required changes in the concept of curriculum. Traditionally, a curriculum was defined in terms of textbook units. For those who were more sophisticated, textbook publishers would supply a series of textbooks designed to lead students through a sequence of progressively more difficult textbooks and assignments. Diagnostic instruction required teachers to think of a curriculum as a collection of units arranged in a hierarchical rather than linear order of difficulty. Beginners learned basic skills while at the same time and in the same classroom more advanced students dealt with more difficult matters. According to the diagnostic approach to instruction, students enter a class with varying amounts of information about a subject. To run all of them through the same progression of skills at the same time ignores this fact. Teachers must learn to recognize these differences in presenting curricula.

The schematic for diagnostic instruction (see Figure 3) is the key to understanding what happened to Shiloh's ES project, which required that teachers replace older teaching roles with newer ones and, at the same time, develop curricula to complement the new roles. These were the kinds of fundamental changes in individual and institutional behavioral patterns that were absent from Lyndon Johnson's Great Society programs.

Wheeler began implementation of his project confident that the failures of other federal efforts would not be repeated in his schools. "I've been told fifty times that it can't be done and I've agreed with them. But we will do it," he told the teachers in August 1973. To meet his goal, Wheeler used a strategy of introducing the faculty to new materials and techniques of instruction in in-service workshops and then demanding changes in their classroom behavior. This strategy was evident in the introduction of four innovations that were to produce changes in instruction, staffing, and curricula.

Figure 3
Schematic for Diagnostic Instruction

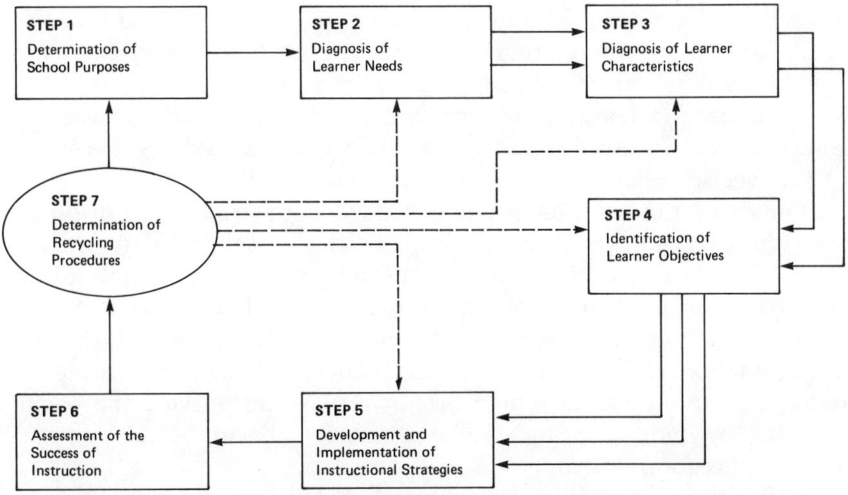

The first innovation was the creation of a diagnostic center, a new facility to be located in the middle school. The center was to be staffed by personnel new to the schools – a reading clinician, reading teachers, an elementary guidance counselor, and a school nurse – with subcontracting for experts in speech and hearing defects, psychological counselors, and social workers. The center's purpose was to diagnose student problems so that classroom teachers could take corrective action.

A second innovation was the insertion of packaged programs into the curriculum. They required teachers to administer tests that purported to diagnose student abilities. Management systems, or subject matter outlines, arranged materials in a hierarchy of difficulty and prescribed specific assignments to correct individual skill deficiencies. Each assignment involved a variety of audiovisual aids, as well as written materials. These packaged programs were intended to redirect classroom behavior to make more efficient learning possible and thereby improve student scores on standardized achievement tests. Thus, the project goal of meeting national test score norms would be met.

A third innovation called for teachers to develop analogues to the packaged programs. Where the programs featured diagnostic testing, teacher observation would be used in the analogues. Where the packaged programs made use of management systems that ran from basic to advanced skills, teachers would create continua of skills. Where packaged programs consisted of tightly knit cognitive units complete with various instructional materials, the teachers would construct learning activity packets (LAPs) that featured the same variety. In both packaged cognitive units and teacher-made LAPs, precise behavioral objectives were specified.

Once the innovations in equipment and materials were in place, Drs. Williams and Jones would explain the principles of diagnostic instruction to the teachers and supply them with the materials necessary to implement this fourth innovation in their classrooms. To support the implementation of diagnostic instruction, Dr. Frankel would analyze and discuss with the teachers videotape recordings of actual classroom events. These discussions would provide the teachers with an understanding of instructional behavior that was beneficial to classroom learning.

This, then, was Wheeler's blueprint for creating the flexible, individualized, instructional program recommended by the independent school survey and funded by the ES project. It was an ambitious plan, aimed directly at changing fundamental classroom behavior on the part of both teachers and students. Since the teachers felt that classroom performance was their legitimate professional concern, they regarded the innovations as interventions which posed a threat to their traditional autonomy. Wheeler's demand that these innovations be adopted set the stage for a struggle over control of the classrooms, a struggle that would ultimately be resolved according to local perceptions of the need for developmental change.

THE DIAGNOSTIC CENTER

The initial in-service workshops held in August 1973 (see Chapter Four) introduced teachers to the diagnostic center, its purposes, and its programs. During the second day of presentations, elementary school teachers met with psychologists hired as consultants to help the teachers deal with problem students. Mr. Beam, one of the psychologists, asked, "Did anyone here not have a problem child last year?" No teacher claimed to have a classroom free of problem children, but one teacher did raise the issue of classroom control.

"Do your analyses always agree with ours?"

"No."

"Then who's right?"

"That's a good question because it leads into who has the authority," said Beam. In the discussion that followed, the teachers insisted that their authority was sovereign in their classrooms. The issue of classroom authority was aired time and again during the year.

Mr. Beam did meet with some success in counseling teachers and parents about problem children. In one elementary school a child balked at coming to school and once there refused to stay. Mr. Beam learned that the child was the youngest of a large family and that his mother was reluctant to have him in school. She told the child that school was a lonely, frightening place and used the child's school behavior to prove her contentions. Mr. Beam told the mother that the child was acting out her fears, not his own, and he suggested that the mother speak positively about school in front of her child. The advice was taken and the child's behavior became acceptable to school personnel.

In another case, Mr. Beam learned that a child's school problems prompted strict discipline measures at home. He advised the teacher to adjust her expectations for the child and to assign tasks the child could manage. Furthermore, the teacher was to send home a daily report on the child's progress. The reports were positive, and discipline at home was replaced by praise. This child's classroom behavior also became acceptable to school personnel and parents.

Despite these successes, the teachers rejected Mr. Beam, saying that his expertise was not helpful and his classroom presence made them nervous. When Wheeler cancelled Mr. Beam's contract, the teachers won a skirmish in the struggle for classroom control.

The August 1973 in-service workshop also introduced teachers to a group of consultants with expertise in speech and hearing disorders. One teacher questioned what he would do with this knowledge. He was told by another to send a child with speech problems to the experts. "Why don't they just say so, then?"

During the 1973-74 school year speech and hearing consultants met with students, but not in the numbers envisioned by Wheeler. Mr. Season brought this up in a meeting with Wheeler and the teachers, saying that he doubted that the center was being used as planned. He asked if the diagnostic center personnel had "ever made a presentation to the board?"

"Not that I know of," said Wheeler.

"It is a key part of diagnostic teaching. The board should have the opportunity to become acquainted with it," said Mr. Season.

"Your problem is that you go around and talk to an individual and are not aware of the total scope. I paid $5,000 last year for [the support services] and not one person here used [them]," argued Wheeler, referring to the teachers in the meeting room.

"The services were there. It was just inconvenient to use them," explained a teacher in support of Wheeler. Others claimed that the teachers were ignorant of the services offered by the center. But there was more to it than this. At first, principals were to take students to the center. They did so with misgivings, viewing the center as an adjunct to the schools, not as the vital part of the system envisioned by the federal project. Wheeler attempted to solve this problem by assigning a center aide the responsibility of chauffeuring elementary students to and from the center. This resulted in greater use of the center but with uneven results. The teachers said the center was one of the best parts of the federal project, because they could send a child there and find out what his or her problems were. But the principals said that even after a problem was diagnosed a teacher might not know what to do with the information.

Wheeler countered Mr. Season's criticism by asserting that during funding negotiations, Washington had deleted the position of center director, resulting in an organizational subsystem with no provision for its management. If the center was less than the federal project called for, it was because Washington had intervened. "They [the ES staff in Washington] have a way of cutting the legs out from under a superintendent," said Wheeler.

PACKAGED PROGRAMS

The second innovation for achieving diagnostic instruction was the introduction of packaged instructional programs. The major programs were in reading and mathematics for grades three through eight. While similar in some respects, the two programs were not equivalent in terms of internal organization. The reading program organized a host of materials in a simple-to-complex skill hierarchy, but the mathematics program did not, which led to differential classroom use.

Reading

The reading program was introduced to teachers during the August 1973 in-service workshop by consultants to the firm that sold the program. All of these consultants had used the reading program in their own schools and thus had practical experience with it. They were scornful of theory, insisting that the reading program would take care of practical reading problems whereas theory was simply talk.

The reading program was akin to an assembly line. Students learned to read by progressing from simple to more complex skills through mastery of all the materials contained in a set of levels (called subsystems). A teacher simply administered a test to place students at the appropriate levels. Then the students were shown how to use the subject matter outline, which guided them through the progression of materials. The teacher then administered tests designed to indicate whether a child knew the content of various assignments. When a test showed a student deficient in a skill, a specific set of materials, matched to the student's level of ability, was prescribed.

The internal organization of the reading program was consistent with the curricular demands of diagnostic instruction. Materials followed a simple-to-complex hierarchy. For example, the reading system offered materials that covered the major categories of (1) word study, (2) vocabulary, (3) comprehension, and (4) study skills. Within each category were minor categories grouped according to skill area and student ability. For example, the first minor category under word study was auditory discrimination. Auditory discrimination was divided into more specific skill listings, called prescriptions, ranked from 01 to 17. A child with problems in auditory discrimination was assigned prescription 01. Prescription 01 included material from five different major reading programs, each of which attacked auditory discrimination problems with different components. If prescription 01 did not solve the student's problem, prescriptions 02 through 17 would. In all, the reading system had 500 such prescriptions.

To ensure that the cycle of individual testing and prescription did not become boring, the new reading system came with a huge selection of paperback readers. Each volume was keyed to a level of difficulty by a color code. Thus, a child who had mastered a set of prescriptions could be assigned a book on his or her individual reading level as a reward. When teachers questioned whether reading could be used as a reward for reading, the consultants explained that this had worked in their schools.

The reading system was based on a philosophy that was to bedevil the teachers for months. They viewed classrooms as composed of one or several groups scattered along a bell-shaped curve of ability. The reading system viewed classrooms as composed of individual students mastering individual prescriptions. In order to use the reading system, teachers had to alter their ideas about both curriculum and student/teacher classroom performance. Nothing in their experience had prepared them for this change, and they were thus apprehensive about the reading program. They claimed that the consultants were telling them to turn students into "robots." One teacher summed up this reaction: "I hope that all the creativity that has been bottled up in reading comes unleashed in my classrooms."

Reading teachers spent the final day of the three-week in-service workshop opening boxes and distributing materials according to the floor plan left by the reading consultants. Some of the teachers were reassured when they got their hands on the materials. "It'll be tough, but we'll do it," said one older teacher who was anxious to implement change in the reading program. However, a younger teacher with a specialty in reading surveyed the mass of materials and wailed, "I don't even know how to teach reading yet. Isn't that a scream? Monday, I'm going to get sixty kids and I don't know how to teach them. I could cry."

Some teachers did cry. It was not uncommon to hear of teachers who had become ill over the demands presented by the new reading program because its management system, the subject matter outline that arranged materials in a hierarchy of difficulty, was still at the printer's office. Teachers had to use a cross-indexed description of materials to write individual prescriptions for children, and this consumed time. One teacher said she was routinely making assignments at midnight for her first morning class.

Wheeler scheduled consultant visits to help overcome these problems. One of the consultants, Ms. Reid, viewed the teachers' reactions without sympathy. She said: "It lets a good teacher go and go, and forces the mediocre teacher to be adequate. Teachers can't fake it with this."

But the teachers could try to avoid using the reading system. During one visit to all the reading centers in Shiloh, Ms. Reid discovered that the Buck Snort reading center was not being used; the materials were still in their packing cases. Reading was being taught as a group activity with individual students reciting from a textbook – just as they had always done. Ms. Reid's recommendations were blunt: strip the teacher of her traditional instructional tools. "Take her books away from her. Make her teach her classes from the [reading system] material." This advice was followed, proving that teachers did not have the power to reject the innovation, not even in Buck Snort, the most isolated school in Shiloh's system.

By December 1973 the reading system was in use throughout the schools. The effects on classroom behavior were dramatic. At the beginning of class, students went to file cabinets to pick up their own record folders and then sought out the materials prescribed for them. Teachers occupied a central station and either checked papers or consulted with students. Each student's needs and abilities were diagnosed, and the student had a specific assignment tailored to meet those needs and abilities.

Although classroom behavior had changed, some teacher attitudes had not. One middle school teacher had a student who was able to read at a minimal level. When the student asked for permission to listen to a set of tapes that explained the printing on an illustrated book, the teacher denied the request. The child immediately went from place to place, disturbing working students at each stop. The teacher threatened the student with physical punishment and said that, while teachers might try new ways of dealing with students, they always returned to the traditional mode because it allowed them greater control over the classroom.

Other faculty members had similar problems. According to one teacher, whom Superintendent Wheeler and Ms. Reid said was successful in implementing the system, "They say this system is teacher-proof, but I can lose a child for days." Contrasting the new system with the older way of teaching, she remarked, "We all feel like we're missing something." The "something" was personal contact with the students. Her principal echoed the complaint. "The thing I don't understand is why don't they just put a computer in the room and do away with teachers? It seems like that's the way it's going."

Thus, the innovation had been introduced, but neither the teaching philosophy it represented nor the change in teacher attitudes it required was accepted in Shiloh's schools. Teachers and principals were not comfortable with a technology that altered fundamental classroom behavior.

The students had another view. Most of them enjoyed the reading program because it offered the illusion of self-direction. During one class a child called out to his teacher, "Dr. Seuss is too hard for me. I'm going to get another book."

Ms. Reid, who witnessed the class, said the child's reaction was typical and related an anecdote to support her contention. She had asked a migrant worker's child how he liked the reading system. "It's okay."

"How's the rest of school?"

"It stinks."

"Why is reading okay when the rest of school stinks?"

"Because there isn't a blankety-blank teacher telling me what to do." (Blankety-blank was Ms. Reid's translation of the boy's description.)

Dramatic proof that the reading system was in good working order came over the 1973 Christmas vacation. Ms. Reid was engaged in a similar project being conducted elsewhere. Mention was made of Shiloh County, and Ms. Reid learned that a teacher would be going to a town near Shiloh for the holidays. She invited the teacher to visit the reading center at the Shiloh County Middle School, saying it was the best center she knew of. A second positive sign came when Ms. Reid asked one of the middle school reading teachers to work for her firm as a consultant to other schools implementing the reading program.

These two events were the teachers' first objective evidence of success. The expectation was that success in implementing the reading system would automatically lead to a gain in student scores in national achievement tests. The expectation was not met, however. In the two-week in-service workshop held during August 1974, Dr. Williams, the consultant for diagnostic instruction, told the assembled teachers that the overall reading achievement test scores had dropped.

The teachers were angered by this news. They had been called upon to implement reading and mathematics programs that created individualized instruction. They had done so, even though they were not in sympathy with the innovation. Now they discovered that the change had not resulted in meeting a project goal. One teacher expressed the reaction succinctly: "He's saying that the teachers are a failure."

The elementary schools teachers believed that the new reading and mathematics programs actually caused the drop in scores. The teachers traditionally relied on competition to motivate students. Introduction of individualized instruction ended competition, because students worked separately on individual assignments. The lack of motivation to excel was thought to explain the drop in scores.

The combination of the drop in scores and teacher responses led Wheeler to allow changes in the reading program during the second year of the federal project. A child was exposed to individualized instruction in the reading center and to small group instruction in the classroom, including individual and group oral delivery. By the end of the second year, reading achievement test scores were close to what they had been before the inception of the federal project, and the teachers claimed that this was due solely to the modification in instructional techniques. They regarded the modification as acquiescence to their demands for professional autonomy in the classroom.

The improvement in achievement test scores did not eliminate teachers' reservations about the reading program. They made this clear in a group discussion at the end of the second year. One teacher said, "I do more clerical work and taking care of discipline problems in the reading center [than teaching]." Another commented, "Some days I don't do any teaching." Still another observed, "Average students and below average cannot work without constant supervision." One teacher said that answers were printed on the back of prescriptions and children simply copied answers rather than doing the prescribed exercises. "We're teaching children to cheat," she said.

Elementary and middle school teachers had used the reading program to change fundamental behaviors in classrooms. The results of such change harmed the students, the teachers claimed, and they cited the initial drop in achievement test scores as evidence of the damage. The improvement in test scores following a return to traditional teaching methods confirmed the teachers' faith in traditional instruction.

Mathematics

The mathematics program for grades three through eight was also introduced to teachers during the August 1973 in-service workshop. The consultants were the program sales representative and several Ph.D.s in mathematics recruited from demonstration projects and State Department of Education offices. Significantly, none of the consultants had ever used the program in classrooms. Their presentations sparked adverse reactions. They were considered to be "smart Yankees" talking down to southern teachers.

The project administration also knew of teacher hostility to the implementation of the new math program.

"How's the program going?" a project coordinator asked me.

"I don't know. Teachers are having a meeting about it. Why don't you ask them?" I said.

"Is their principal with them?"

"Yes."

"I thought you were telling me we had a rebellion."

The initial workshop revealed a sharp divergence of expectations concerning the new math program. Wheeler said that the new materials would lead to students' meeting national norms on standardized achievement tests in mathematics, but the consultants publicly denied the program's score-raising potential, saying that the goal of their program was to individualize instruction. Individualization would make school a more pleasant place for students by ending the risk of failure, but it would also lead to a drop in math achievement test scores because students would not work as hard individually as they would in groups. The consultants also predicted a drop in reading scores because of the new reading system. Individualized instruction was the wrong mechanism for raising scores.

Wheeler countered this view in a private session with the math program sales representative. He told the salesman of the national publicity the project would stimulate; he was relying on packaged programs to meet project goals. "If I go down, you go down with me," he said.

The teachers soon discovered that the math program's management system resembled the reading system's management system only superficially. Instead of a hierarchy of skills, the math program contained prescriptions that grouped similar kinds of problems, but problem solving called for much different skills. Furthermore, teachers denounced the management system supplied by the publisher as inadequate.

The teachers asked the salesman to refer them to a school system that had implemented the program. Referred to a nearby system, they found that the math program there was being used in only one classroom, rather than throughout the system, and only as a supplement to textbook assignments.

By the spring of 1974 the math program had suffered different fates in the elementary and middle schools. Elementary school teachers used the program either as basic instructional technology or as a supplement to textbooks. However, middle school teachers would neither accept the innovation in its entirety nor use it as an instructional supplement. They insisted that the program's usefulness was a function of the level of skill difficulty involved. In the elementary schools children learned basic mathematical operations for which the program provided drill material. Middle school teachers taught more complex mathematical skills, which the program could not handle. Furthermore, individualized instruction allowed students to progress at their own rates, which encouraged "goofing off," and the math program's prescriptions contained the answers to problems, so that the children could simply copy the answers without performing the necessary drill. The teachers saw student copying as cheating, an affront to their professional authority.

Wheeler scheduled an in-service math workshop for the end of the 1973-74 school year. It featured a company representative and two university consultants, Drs. Morris and Chalmers, who had expertise in elementary mathematics instruction.

The company representative began by complimenting the middle school teachers: "I would venture to say that there is not another teacher that uses [the math program] that has done the work you've done." The problem was that "you were probably told wrong about placement [i.e., the management system]. [The math program] is a management system, but it won't stand on its own." The company representative claimed that the math program had been organized in accordance with the recommendations of a national council of mathematics teachers.

"Not so," said Dr. Morris, who was a member of that council and claimed that the math program did not conform to the council's recommendations. "I hate to see people sold a bill of goods on half truths, evasions, and misconceptions," said Dr. Morris.

The company representative left the workshop, and Drs. Morris and Chalmers took over. They proposed constructing a skills hierarchy for their own math program. This would return control of the classroom to the teachers. Dr. Morris was not impressed with the claim that the packaged materials are teacher-proof. "Let's reassure ourselves that the things we are doing aren't that bad," said Dr. Morris. He stressed the role that teachers had to play in the classroom. "No book, no abacus, no set of cards is any substitute for what you do as a teacher."

The in-service math workshop concentrated on constructing a minimum set of objectives for guiding math teachers in Shiloh County's elementary and middle schools. By the end of this workshop teachers had an outline of mathematics skills arranged in a hierarchy of difficulty. Their task was to determine each student's appropriate placement in this sequence at grade one and to continue using the outline through grade eight. The math program now had a management system, but it was impossible to tell if there was any classroom carry-over. In the 1974-75 school year the packaged math program was again used in the elementary schools but not in the middle school. Classroom behavior continued as before: students were exposed to group instruction and to small group drill on specific skills. Furthermore, Drs. Morris and Chalmers's management system was used with teacher discretion. As one teacher said, the management system "will go in a desk drawer where I'll forget about it." Teachers were once again controlling their classrooms.

The extent of this control and the localization it implied were demonstrated in an in-service math workshop held at the beginning of the 1975-76 school year. Dr. Morris worked with a group of elementary and middle school teachers. He said that another group of teachers had constructed a set of diagnostic tests to match the management system's minimal objectives for June. "It looks like all we have to do is just extend [the diagnostic tests to cover the middle school]," said Dr. Morris.

"I don't know what they got done," said a middle school teacher, indicating that the effort was not systemwide.

"They got the whole thing done. There's no point in redoing what's already been done," said Dr. Morris.

"I've never seen it. I wish we had a copy," said the middle school teacher.

Dr. Morris explained the diagnostic tests. The teachers had constructed five test items for each minimal objective in the management system. The tests were to be given to all the students in a class. Any student who missed two of the five items needed to do more work in that specific skill. Through repeated testing, a teacher could create skill groups and place each child in a group according to the proper level of difficulty. "You can't teach masses of children as a tutorial," said Dr. Morris. Diagnostic testing allowed the teacher to "see . . . the strengths and weaknesses of each kid . . . and then begin to group."

"You have to have a stack of tests this thick," protested a middle school teacher holding his hands apart.

"That's the way it is when you start diagnostic testing and teaching," Dr. Morris replied. Again, it was difficult to tell if there was classroom carry-over from this workshop.

A basic mathematics program used in the high school consisted of an integrated set of individualized materials; students were expected to follow a management system that took them from simple to complex skills. A student who failed to master a set of skills was to call upon the teacher for help. But there was an organizational problem in this plan, for the program had to serve sixty students and two teachers in one of the semiopen classrooms in the new high school. As classroom managers the teachers were unable to assist individual students in a timely fashion. Student dissatisfaction with the arrangement led to a strike which lent further support to the teachers' resistance to individualized instruction.

On October 8, 1974, thirty-five students left the high school in protest over school conditions. Three students said the strike was called to protest rules. "You've got to have a note to go to the can." But there was more to it than that. The students disliked the new roles their teachers were playing in the classrooms. Wheeler met the students in the high school parking lot and persuaded them to return to the commons area to discuss problems. The conversations focused on the math program and teacher attitudes. "Some of these teachers act like they own you," said a striker.

"All I've got to do to make you all happy is fire six teachers," said Wheeler.

"No. It's not all the teachers. It's just a few of them," said a striker.

Wheeler countered with a chain-of-command argument that supported the principle of obedience to rules – the same argument that his teachers used to justify their resistance to individualized instruction. "For the rest of your life, you're going to have to deal with authority. When you walked out that door, you broke a school rule," said Wheeler.

A student voiced Shiloh's decision-making tradition. All leaders had to consult with their followers. "This is like a factory, isn't it? When the employees go on strike, they don't fire them. They listen to them."

Responding to continued complaints about school rules, Collins, the high school principal, echoed Wheeler's argument. "That's the only way I know to run an orderly school." One striker did not buy the argument. He left the discussion group, telling Wheeler, Collins, and the students, "You all failed me."

A strike organizer later said, "I like school okay. It's the teachers' attitudes I don't like." He described the basic math program as the greatest problem: there were too many students in class, they had to stand in line to consult with teachers, teachers constantly told students to "shut up," different teachers invaded semiopen classroom spaces and gave students different orders, and students had no help in solving math problems. The striker said that the next step would be "to take it to court."

But court was not the next step. The next step was to confront the board. A student delegation, composed of nonstriking students and accompanied by one parent, came to the next scheduled board meeting. Complaints about the math program were foremost. Said one student, "We were led to believe that the work would be individualized. But they have a goal of how many you're supposed to do. You have to get so many done for a C or a D . . . . If you're sick . . . I talked to [a teacher] and he said, 'It's your tough luck.' "

The students considered this attitude unfair. "The reason you are there is because you don't know how. Unless you already know it before, there is no way you can get it. I admit [the teachers] try to help you, but they can't get around to each student. They just don't have enough time to do what they are supposed to do."

The same teachers behaved differently in other classrooms where they followed traditional teaching models. "Fifth period is algebra. They've got a book and [the teacher] explains it." There was no book for basic math. "It's the system. It's just no good. We're trying a lot of new things and a lot of them aren't going to work in our schools."

Abuse of authority was cited as another problem. "Some of the teachers just have the power. They . . . feel like students should bow down to them. I'd like to see what would happen to a student who told his teacher to shut up. They'd get flattened. I might be wrong, but I always thought that the schools were for the students."

The delegation claimed to represent the student body. "There was really supposed to be a lot more people here, but they ran out on us. The main portion of the school has a complaint. We're just here representing it. I think at least 75 percent of the students are behind us."

A board member protested, "As policymakers we can't solve your problems."

"Who do we talk to?"

"Any society has to have rules and regulations. If you don't, you go back to 'might makes right', " said Wheeler.

"We just want to change some rules," protested a student.

"You always operate within the system," Wheeler insisted.

"You're creating a problem and problems create restrictions," observed a board member.

"The minute we give in," added Wheeler.

"We're not going to give in to anyone who walks out," a board member declared.

Wheeler had another worry – that the student strike would lead to community intervention in support of the students. "You know this is going to be reported tomorrow," said Wheeler.

"What do you mean?" asked a student.

"On the radio."

"The more the better," said the student because he wanted to attract the attention of community members and get them to intervene on the students' behalf.

The public encounter ended and the student delegation left. Wheeler then acknowledged that his federal program might be at fault for the strike. "To tell the truth, we need to look at the math program – maybe."

"That's no excuse for them walking out," said a board member, ignoring the fact that it was a public demonstration to put the problems created by the federal project before the board. Another board member agreed with his peer. At issue was not this or that program, but political power. "Either we run it or they run it," he said.

Wheeler talked all the striking students into returning to school for economic reasons: the state supported Shiloh's educational system by paying about $2.75 per day for each child who attended, so Wheeler needed the disaffected children in school. "Do you know what forty kids are worth?" he asked.

But Wheeler's resolution of the strike undermined the teachers' classroom authority. They said that Wheeler had taken the strikers for "a ride in his big car" and talked them into returning without imposing penalties for the walkout. His actions left teachers "without a leg to stand on" because their authority had been overridden. The teachers had used the math program technology to change classroom behavior. The results had been disastrous. Students were unhappy about classroom conditions and wanted a return to more traditional teaching methods. The teachers' faith in traditional instruction was thus reconfirmed.

Teacher-Related Curricula

The third innovation for implementing diagnostic instruction was the creation of learning activity packets to be used by secondary school teachers for reading and math instruction. During the initial in-service workshop in August 1973, Drs. Millsap and Lampkin instructed teachers in creating LAPs. Equivalent to prescriptions in a packaged program, each LAP integrated a number of different learning activities to meet a clearly stated instructional goal. Table 1 gives a general outline for a LAP.

Table 1
Outline for a Learning Activity Packet

I. Title
II. Rationale
III. Objectives
  A. Learning
  B. Performance objectives (student's demonstration of learning)
IV. Pretest
V. List of Learning Activities
VI. Postevaluation
VII. Quest Activities

Drs. Millsap and Lampkin emphasized that the most important elements of LAPs were the learning and performance objectives, the instructional technologies that allowed for varied but coordinated learning activities, and postevaluation. The title, rationale, pretest, and quest activities were less important.

Drs. Millsap and Lampkin were also specific about the aim of teacher-created materials: LAPs would form a continuum from simple to complex skills along which students could progress. The specific cognitive units in continua provided secondary teachers with the equivalent of packaged curricula. Wheeler stressed this when he told teachers that the federal program had supplied packaged programs for elementary school teachers, but that the secondary school teachers would have to create programs and were thus "paying a higher price for change."

The goal of all this teacher activity in shaping curricula was bluntly stated by Dr. Millsap in the initial in-service workshop. He said that college preparation and textbook-oriented schools had trained teachers not to make decisions about curricula. Creation of LAPs would force them to make such decisions and would thus wean teachers from dependence on textbooks, unit assignments, and group activities.

The principals were not keen about LAPs. They said that teachers were not learning anything new in the in-service workshops. Lesson plans were part of teacher training in college, yet when teachers went into classrooms they discarded lesson plans. Collins was afraid the same would happen to LAPs. "If we don't individualize instruction, we're not doing anything. It looks good on paper, but the trouble is in implementing it. It's going to require lots of supervision."

The secondary school teachers complained that education moves in cycles, each with its own jargon and technical fads. Individualized instruction and LAPs were simply the crest of the current cycle. One teacher protested, "This attack on textbooks is the craziest thing I ever heard of."

Introduction of LAPs and curriculum continua went through several stages. In the first stage Drs. Lampkin and Millsap talked about LAP construction. They assumed that the teachers wanted to change classroom behavior and would utilize paid in-service time and consultant expertise to write the cognitive units that would allow them to do so. This assumption was proved false during the February 15, 1974, in-service workshop. An assistant superintendent whose wife taught in the high school said, "All the high school program amounts to is a bunch of bullshit." The teachers agreed and complained that they were being "kicked around [and] treated like stepchildren." When Dr. Millsap asked how many LAPs each teacher had constructed, he was told, "None."

The workshop broke for lunch. When it reconvened the teachers were divided into task "groups" of one member each and told by Dr. Millsap that each teacher was responsible for creating LAPs. The teachers recognized the strategy behind this statement. "Teachers are just like students. They won't work unless someone forces them to," said one middle school teacher.

They resisted this new task-group structure and sought community support for their protest. A concerned citizen later criticized the workshop, saying that it did not benefit the teachers, but merely met the contractual obligation between the school district and the ES office in Washington. The content and structure of the workshops should be negotiated between teachers and administrators rather than established by administrative fiat. This citizen said that he was interested in creating a dialogue between Wheeler and the teachers. He later contacted the *Shiloh Crier* – not to seek publication of his views, he said, but to provide background information.

Thus, the teachers were using Shiloh's communal frames of reference to create political alliances that would help them curb Wheeler.

In the next in-service workshop one-member task groups were again formed. First, however, Wheeler gave a thirty-minute speech to the teachers:

> The theory behind this whole in-service workshop is that the teacher will know curriculum and can put it down in a form that a kid can work out by himself or with others. We've thrown a lot at you and you've responded well. All that I'm asking of you is to relax. It's not that difficult. We've got a good faculty. The only criticism I can offer is you see things as a life and death situation. It isn't. Don't put all this tension on yourself.

Dr. Millsap then took over the workshop. Handing a slip of paper to each teacher, he asked that they record their names and the number of LAPs they had constructed. "Mr. Wheeler wants it. Isn't that right?" asked Dr. Millsap.

"That's right," said Wheeler.

A teacher laughed and said her colleagues had given her excellent advice. They had told her, "Don't be a fool. Give the man what he wants and then do as you please." Superintendent Wheeler and Dr. Millsap could dictate in-service task groupings and formal content, but they could not dictate teachers' responses to their demands.

The two men lost control of the task groups during the workshop. Teachers were allowed to work on the LAPs in their classrooms because "that's where their materials are." During the time scheduled for the workshop they talked with their friends. The only apparent concern with LAPs was demonstrated when Dr. Millsap visited with teacher groups; when he left, LAP construction ended. Thus, the formal content of in-service sessions was beyond the control of the two men.

However, accountability procedures were not relaxed. In one of the last workshops of the 1973-74 school year, Drs. Lampkin and Millsap passed out forms that asked each teacher how many LAPs they had completed, how many were under construction, and how many were planned. They described the form as "a little test." The teachers used more profane terms.

Mr. Season visited the site in time to witness the September 25, 1974, workshop. He asked the secondary school teachers if they were using LAPs and, if so, if he might see examples of them. He later said that the LAPs he saw were miniature textbooks, not alternative instructional strategies. Dr. Millsap agreed:

> I'm not really surprised at what you found. These teachers adjust – some of these teachers. They have just got to realize that there are different techniques of teaching other than standardizing their presentation. To individualize, you've got to have a wider repertoire of instructional strategies. You know, we have been talking about changing their teaching behavior and this is difficult.

Immediately following this conversation, Mr. Season, Dr. Millsap, and Superintendent Wheeler joined the workshop group in the commons area. Wheeler took the floor to tell the teachers that Mr. Season "has been concerned about our LAPs." But that was not quite the whole truth, for as Ms. Season later said of Shiloh's project:

> Their main thing was diagnostic instruction, or diagnostic teaching. And they weren't clear in the beginning what that meant. One of the strategies that they worked on to get at diagnostic instruction was the writing of learning activity packets. They brought in a consultant. Either he didn't know what he was talking about, or he wasn't able to get it across, or the teachers weren't taking it too seriously. I suppose that if I had never had any experience with LAPs myself, I wouldn't have known a good one from a bad one. And it would have continued the way it was because the superintendent didn't seem to know the difference.

There were other voices to be heard from – those of the teachers. One teacher who showed samples of her LAPs to Mr. Season said that his concerns were his problem. "I'm a dedicated, conscientious teacher. I don't care if I don't have it written right." Another teacher who had witnessed the exchange between Mr. Season, Dr. Millsap, and Superintendent Wheeler said that Wheeler's performance "was just bullshit. It's pitiful. If they [i.e., Mr. Season] can't see through that, they're pitiful."

The teachers disliked the LAPs because paper and pencil performance created too much paperwork. With a departmentalized organizational structure, each teacher taught nearly 100 students per day. One teacher estimated that she had received 1,120 different written returns on one LAP alone. "I went back to the old way," she said.

But LAPs were used in some classrooms. This gave the middle and high schools two different forms of student/teacher relationships. Some classrooms operated like the reading centers: teachers sat at a central station, either correcting papers or counseling individual students, and the students completed individual assignments prescribed in the LAPs. Drs. Lampkin and Millsap said that LAPs had been accepted in these classrooms. In other classrooms teachers produced miniature textbooks. Students remained at their desks, completing assignments that had been given as a group activity. Drs. Lampkin and Millsap said that instruction in these classrooms was better than it had been prior to the federal project, but the consultants were not inclined to brag about the results.

Teacher interviews showed a range of attitudes that matched the range of classroom behavior. In those classrooms where students were meeting performance objectives independently, the teachers said that sharing written assignments equaled diagnostic instruction. In classrooms where teachers used LAPs as textbooks, the teachers did not think the instruction differed from traditional modes. As one teacher observed, "All teachers teach units. I'm just pulling mine together and calling them LAPs."

A final perspective should be mentioned. Secondary school students resented the federal project and its innovations. One said the entire Experimental Schools program made him "feel like a guinea pig." Others said that LAPs stood between them and their teachers. The LAP-induced disruption of fundamental classroom behaviors led to a widespread student complaint in the high school: "Our teachers don't like us anymore." A teacher remarked, "These kids don't want LAPs. They want somebody to teach them something." Once again, the teachers reconfirmed their belief that individualizing instruction, and thereby changing fundamental classroom behavior, harmed students, and student complaints supported this conviction.

DIAGNOSTIC INSTRUCTION

In a meeting held on June 1, 1975, Dr. Williams defined diagnostic instruction as an approach that "assumes that the teacher has to understand the learner's needs and learning styles (diagnosis) before structuring relevant and meaningful learning opportunities for the learner (prescription)." Almost two years earlier, Wheeler had introduced a workshop on diagnostic instruction as follows:

> We're involved in a four-year project. Whether we succeed or fail will be determined in the next three months. Make no mistake about that. If you don't understand diagnostic instruction in the in-service workshop, the project is a failure. I can't emphasize to you the importance of the in-service workshop for the next three months.

Events occurring between these two meetings generated a great deal of conflict among the teachers, Superintendent Wheeler, and Drs. Williams and Jones. At issue were fundamental changes in individual classroom behavior.

Drs. Williams and Jones then took the floor. Referring to the diagram of diagnostic instruction distributed to the teachers (see Figure 3), they said that each school faculty should define its school's purpose. They passed out decks of cards with printed statements on them to each faculty group and asked the groups to order the statements in terms of priorities. All agreed on the first two:

1. To develop self-concepts and behaviors consistent with capabilities and desirable human relationships in school, the family, and with all other people.
2. To develop a desire to pursue learning interests for the joy and sense of accomplishment in learning.

Dr. Jones viewed the teachers' selection of school priorities with disdain. Concern with self-concept was not something that teachers should worry about: they were in school to teach, not to provide social services. Dr. Jones illustrated his point by relating an anecdote. He knew a teacher who got along well with his students. One student, whose father was in prison, showed his teacher a wallet that his father had made in the prison craft center. The child promised his teacher, "When I grow up and go to prison, I'll make you a wallet." So much for molding the child's self-concept.

The initial disagreement between Dr. Jones and the teachers on priorities was widened in another workshop. Teachers were broken into task groups of school faculties and taken into separate rooms. After presentations by Drs. Williams and Jones, the entire faculty reassembled in the commons area. The teachers expected to be asked for group consensus on discussions, but instead they were asked to volunteer information as individuals. None did. The teachers later recalled that Dr. Jones said, "If you don't want to talk, to hell with you."

Despite disagreement between teachers and consultants, the workshop continued. One session focused on the fourth step in the schematic: identification of learner objectives. A standard taxonomy of objectives was copied from an educational textbook and passed out to the teaching staff. The teachers were puzzled by the taxonomy; when Drs. Williams and Jones asked them to list the objectives from memory, the teachers merely copied the list on a separate piece of paper – exactly as students answered questions in the packaged reading and math programs.

Drs. Williams and Jones then divided the teachers into two groups. One group, under Dr. Jones's tutelage, adjourned to the media center and listened as he tried to translate the taxonomy of learner objectives into simpler terms. Finally a teacher said that she could not apply the taxonomy to the schematic and arrive at anything useful for her classes. Dr. Jones asked why she had not said so before.

"I'm dumb. But I don't want to seem dumber," she said.

"You may be dumb, but you've got guts," said another teacher, and the issue of diagnostic instruction was debated.

Other teachers supported the objector. One said that departmentalization forced her to teach a new set of students each period. No teacher could use diagnostic instruction when faced with 8 classes per day and 450 students per week.

Dr. Jones abandoned the topic of learner objectives to explain the idea behind diagnostic instruction. He started by saying that teachers see their classes as composed of subgroups based on ability. Each subgroup represents a position on a bell-shaped curve of ability. Diagnostic instruction, in contrast, begins with the idea that classrooms are full of individual students who should be grouped on the basis of individual needs, interests, and abilities so that all students master specific skills in a classroom of interacting peers.

To make his point clearer, Dr. Jones drew an analogy between a classroom of students and an athletic team. "Football and basketball coaches have been using diagnostic instruction for years and years. Show me a winning coach and I'll show you a superb diagnostician." Specification of learner objectives was important because "if you don't know what you want your kids to learn, you can't diagnose." A teacher began to cry, which ended this part of the workshop.

Dr. Williams later prevailed upon Wheeler to relax the pressure on the teachers attending the workshops. Wheeler did so by telling the teachers:

> Until we can get diagnostic instruction into a form that's meaningful to you, let's forget about it. We've got two years. The programs are good. We're making progress. But we've got three years for diagnostic instruction.

That was the end of Wheeler's three-month deadline for mastering diagnostic instruction. The teachers were able to resist an innovation that they saw as eroding their professional status.

Yet the emphasis on diagnostic instruction persisted as Drs. Williams and Jones discussed the role of the learner's emotions. They said that whenever a teacher made a difference to a child, it was because the teacher made use of a child's affective domain. To do this, a teacher had to be able to identify a learner's needs and learning styles – integral steps in the diagnostic instruction schematic. According to Wheeler, the teachers now had the expertise to manipulate both curriculum and learning characteristics. "We've reached the point . . . where you know what you're talking about." The materials provided by the federal project were just tools that would help teachers use their students' affective domains. "Make no mistake about it. The teacher is the curriculum." But the teacher was the curriculum only when he or she exercised traditional professional autonomy.

The next in-service workshop demonstrated that the teachers retained their autonomy, even in the face of pressure to change their role. The workshop focused on constructing learner continua – an integrated set of learning objectives on a hierarchical scale. The first part of the workshop demonstrated that teachers did not grasp the difference between a traditional scope-and-sequence outline of cognitive units and the new arrangement. During a coffee break the elementary school teachers said that the packaged programs provided learner continua and diagnostic testing; they felt they had nothing to learn from further presentations.

When the workshop reconvened, the teachers discovered that what had appeared to be a solid front presented by Wheeler and the consultants was really the result of Wheeler juggling several ill-informed consultants to get the results that he wanted. Wheeler said that he could not solve the problems raised by his teachers. If they wanted a scope-and-sequence outline, the easiest way was to use a textbook. A teacher could supplement the curriculum for slow students or enrich it for the exceptional child. Either way, the teacher was diagnosing student needs and achieving the goal of the federal project.

Wheeler insisted that there was a difference between the diagnostic testing of packaged programs and diagnostic instruction, but his explanation of that difference did not enlighten his teachers:

> I've bet my personal reputation that the Shiloh County staff can come up with that extra that makes you use professional judgment. I want teacher input, but I want constructive input. We'll have a good reading program. We'll have a good math program. Whatever else comes out depends on your effort.

Then Wheeler abandoned the aggressive role he had adopted in introducing the faculty to instructional changes, saying, "I see absolutely no hope. I see no hope." Wheeler had done his share by providing the money, materials, and consultant expertise. The teachers were not carrying their part of the burden in the change process.

All the consultants – Drs. Williams, Jones, Millsap, and Lampkin – disagreed with Wheeler. They believed there was a way to meet the problems raised by the teachers, but they could not immediately say what it was. Wheeler played devil's advocate by debating with his consultants. The encounter fed teacher confusion and disaffection. One teacher said, "It was embarrassing. I didn't know what to do." Another said that there was no difference between a traditional scope-and-sequence outline and a learning continuum – Wheeler simply needed a new word to dress up an old method in order to please Washington. A third said, "All I hear is it's something we've been doing all along."

This set of events crystallized attitudes and was thus a turning point in the project. Changes in classroom behavior demanded an integration of new teaching models and new curricula. Yet the teachers did not grasp the difference between old and new curricula, and their leader could not explain the difference. Wheeler's role as devil's advocate not only destroyed his credentials as an educational leader introducing innovative changes, it also exposed his consultants' disorganization. All that Wheeler could do was to appeal to the teachers' loyalty in an effort to salvage his personal reputation.

The next workshop featured a new plan for getting teachers to specify learner objectives. Teachers were broken into task groups;

each group was led by a principal who was responsible for creating a learning continuum for a specific cognitive area. Once this was accomplished, the teachers could concentrate on creating LAPs that met the learner objectives specified in the continuum. After developing curricula, the teachers would be supplied with a set of forms created by Drs. Williams and Jones to ensure that diagnostic instruction was implemented in all classrooms. The strategy for changing individual and institutional behavior had finally been given a clear form: first integrate specific materials into the instructional subsystem, then concentrate on altering classroom performance.

Things did not work as planned. Drs. Williams and Jones were enlisted in the two-week in-service workshop preceding the 1974-75 school year to tell the teachers that achievement test scores had fallen. This led to considerable disquiet among the teachers, which was aggravated when Drs. Williams and Jones introduced a set of forms for each teacher to keep on one class during the first nine-week period of instruction.

The forms were contained in a "blue book," a loose-leaf binder with a blue cover. Each blue book held four types of forms to be filled out for each student. The first form was the student assignment record (time and content of the assignment, method of instruction, and method of evaluation); the second was the student diagnostic record (student's reinforcement source, learning style, and other comments); the third was the diagnostic record of continuum needs; and the fourth was a record of instructional strategies (grouping, materials, special assistance, and so forth). As these forms were passed out to the teachers, Dr. Jones said, "If you're not ready now, you never will be."

Wheeler took the floor to comment on the blue book: "As most of you are aware, we have an Experimental Schools program. As most of you are aware, one of its shortcomings is a record-keeping system on an individual basis." The blue book would remedy this defect by extending Wheeler's federal plan for changing behavior into every classroom in Shiloh County. "It's a lot of work, but it's necessary. It's an attempt to get diagnostic teaching firmly entrenched in your philosophy. This is the year of the crunch," warned Wheeler.

The teachers responded immediately. "How do you individualize instruction?"

"You don't. You just do better at it than you did last year. I know as well as you that complete individualization is a gross impossibility. It's the better we are after, not the absolute. This is better than writing lesson plans and submitting them in advance." said Dr. Williams.

"You're writing thirty lesson plans," said a teacher.

Superintendent Wheeler and Drs. Williams and Jones said that they assumed there was an agreement between themselves and the teaching staff: the teachers would keep records in the blue book for the first nine-week class period. The teachers knew no such agreement existed. They did not, they said, have the time to keep the number of records required.

The assumption that such an agreement existed led to a set of explosive encounters when Drs. Williams and Jones addressed the teaching staff nine weeks later. The workshop in which these encounters occurred was held in two different locations: secondary school teachers met with Dr. Jones in the commons area of the high school while elementary school teachers met with Dr. Williams in the Clarksville Elementary School. The secondary school teachers' workshop started with a speech by Wheeler on the necessity of keeping blue book records. "It assures the administration, the board, that every student [in grades] one through twelve is looked at as an individual and I don't know of another system that does that."

Dr. Jones took the floor. "How many of you see a parallel between diagnostic instruction and your in-service workshop?" No teacher answered. "This is the kind of thing we are trying to get away from in the classroom," said Dr. Jones. He asked another question and received no answer.

"Are they being polite and kind? Or are they just habitual liars?" he asked Wheeler.

Dr. Jones again asked the teachers a question and again received no response. "How did I turn you off so fast? Do I sound like a Sunday School teacher?" No one answered, but one teacher started to raise an arm. "Do you have a question?"

"No. I've decided [remaining silent is] the best policy," said the teacher.

"Why do we have to write it down?" asked another teacher. (At this point Wheeler left to take part in the elementary school teachers' workshop.)

"One of the reasons is that most of the teachers in the past have planned one activity for the entire class," explained Dr. Jones.

A teacher said that she routinely planned different activities for different children in her class and kept records in her planning book.

She showed the planning book to Dr. Jones. Several teachers complained that they were tired of hearing what was wrong with the Shiloh County teaching staff. They routinely did the required things and gained no recognition for this. Dr. Jones agreed that many things were done well in Shiloh County and apologized for not mentioning them. This did not satisfy one teacher, who said that the teachers had no use for the consultants who were in Shiloh County, only for the money provided by the federal project.

"Have I preached a sermon?" asked Dr. Jones.

"Yes."

"Let's say benediction and go home," quipped a teacher.

"How many of you are using the blue book?" asked Dr. Jones. No one was. "I came here assuming that everyone was complying with the agreement we made last August. One thing I learned tonight is to make certain I know what's going on before I make a damned fool of myself," said Dr. Jones.

The teachers made a point of ignoring Dr. Jones. They turned to their neighbors and engaged in private conversations. Dr. Jones threatened to tell Wheeler that the teachers were not willing to continue with the federal program and that the schools should withdraw from it. "It's pretty embarrassing to stand here with your bare face hanging out," he said. The teachers continued to ignore him. "I can't work like this," he said, and the workshop ended.

In the meantime, Wheeler had a confrontation with Dr. Williams at the workshop for elementary school teachers. Wheeler took the floor to castigate the staff for their "constant negativism." Dr. Williams said that he had not noticed any negativism until Wheeler joined the workshop. The teachers supported Dr. Williams. "He took up for the teachers," they said.

Dr. Williams later summed up his reaction to the workshop: "It got pretty hairy . . . [but] everything has worked itself out. We can't be change agents directly. There's nothing we can give other than a loose intellectual mode." A group of teachers whom Wheeler, the project coordinators, and the consultants deemed successful in implementing diagnostic instruction were chosen as the agents of change. These teachers represented all departments in the schools and were paid a higher salary to be exemplary teachers.

A meeting was held on November 4, 1974, between the exemplary teachers and Drs. Williams and Jones. The meeting did not bode well for further classroom change. "I take it there's no problems," said Dr. Williams. The teachers were silent.

"Where do you go from here?" asked Dr. Jones.

"I hope nowhere," said a teacher.

That was the life and death of the new tactic for changing classroom behavior. Drs. Williams and Jones withdrew from active participation in promoting change, which was what the teachers wanted. One teacher who had led the assault on Dr. Jones said, "We gave him both barrels. We ran him off."

One further attempt at innovation should be mentioned here. In order to support diagnostic instruction, the federal project proposed to use Dr. Frankel's videotape recordings and analysis of classroom activities to instruct teachers in the techniques of behavior modification.

Dr. Frankel did not fare well in Shiloh County. At first, he and his colleague, Dr. Ribbon, did not have access to the videotape equipment they needed. Their first class therefore centered on theory, not practice, and the teachers said the results were not worthwhile. Perhaps it was this experience that led Dr. Ribbon to withdraw from the project.

When the videotape machines arrived, the program continued under Dr. Frankel's leadership. During an in-service workshop held for elementary school teachers, participants learned what the program offered them, and they were not impressed with what they stood to gain. One teacher recalled the first workshop and said, "It'll be the same as it was last time." Another teacher complained that Dr. Frankel's presentation was "too quick . . . . I couldn't catch it." A third said that Dr. Frankel was "out of it."

These attitudes were relayed to Wheeler. Just before the next workshop, he told Dr. Frankel, "Pep it up tonight."

"From what angle?" asked Dr. Frankel, but Wheeler did not reply.

During the in-service workshop, the teachers expressed their opposition to the program in a variety of ways. One teacher asked, "What situations do you tape in?"

"Use the average child," said Dr. Frankel.

"We don't have too many of those," said a teacher. Another teacher refused to be televised, claiming the camera distorted her figure. A third teacher confronted the innovation directly. "If I'm correct, Mr. Wheeler said we'd ask for volunteers. If we didn't want to volunteer, we didn't have to."

"Are you trying to tell us you won't volunteer?" asked a graduate student who was helping Dr. Frankel during this workshop.

"That is correct."

The teachers' resistance to what they considered a technological invasion of their classrooms led Wheeler to admit, "It just didn't work at the elementary level."

The innovation also failed in the middle school. The teachers had learned that if they refused to respond to Dr. Frankel's questions, he would run out of things to say. "We're more than a little hostile," admitted one teacher.

Teacher reaction led Dr. Frankel to acknowledge that his program was not applicable to Shiloh's schools. During the workshop of December 8, 1974, he said that complaints about the amount of time his program consumed were accurate. "It's just incomprehensible how you could spend time, energy, and resources on just a few kids generated across a large number." Thereafter, the videotape machines were used to tape athletic events and programs on educational television.

ACTUAL CHANGES IN INSTITUTIONAL AND INDIVIDUAL BEHAVIOR

Institutional Changes

Very little was changed at the program level as a result of Shiloh's ES project. The diagnostic center became an adjunct to the schools and not the vital part of individualized instruction envisioned in the ES plan. The reading program replaced group instruction during the first year but merely supplemented traditional teaching methods during the second year, because the teachers claimed that individualized instruction led to decreased reading achievement scores. The math program in grades three through eight was abandoned because of teacher frustration, and its replacement, the program furnished by Drs. Chalmers and Morris, was not universally implemented in Shiloh's classrooms. The basic math program in the high school replaced traditional teaching, helped foster a student rebellion, and led Wheeler to behave in ways that the teachers saw as threatening. Learning activity packets did individualize instruction in some classrooms, but for the most part teachers used LAPs as miniature textbooks. Curriculum continua did not replace the older scope-and-sequence organization because teachers could not distinguish between the two. Diagnostic instruction did not replace the older idea of group instruction because teachers feared that implementing diagnostic instruction would lessen both their classroom authority and their students' learning. Finally, teacher hostility led Dr. Frankel to admit that his program of behavior modification was not applicable to Shiloh's classrooms.

Individual Changes

Just as Shiloh's ES project brought only minor changes at the program level, it produced no fundamental changes in individual behavior. Students and teachers both learned new ways to act in the classroom, but their new behaviors augmented rather than replaced traditional roles. In the reading centers teachers became classroom managers and students became independent learners, but upon their return to regular classrooms, more traditional roles were assumed. The innovations that were intended to promote the reading center type of behavior in the classrooms – learning activity packets, curriculum continua, and diagnostic instruction – did not work as planned.

What, then, were the fundamental changes in individual and institutional behavior attributable to Shiloh's ES project? There were none, save in a few isolated classrooms. The reactions of both teachers and students obstructed Wheeler's attempts to impose behavioral change. Shiloh's ES project, therefore, had only limited impact on fundamental classroom behavior.

Notes

1. Schultze et al., *Setting National Priorities,* p. 452.
2. Ibid., p. 453.

6

Community Agendas for Developmental Change in Shiloh's Schools

While Wheeler's ability to forge a systemic linkage, his style of leadership, and his planning and implementation of developmental change were sufficient to mollify the ES office in Washington, they were not sufficient to satisfy certain community agendas for developmental change in Shiloh's schools. These agendas were based on the desire for equity: Cuba Landing and South Shiloh wanted school facilities comparable with those in Clarksville. When Wheeler's building plans appeared to run counter to community desires, Shiloh's political processes were put in motion to stop them.

A major confrontation with a community group began with Wheeler's interpretation of a building recommendation contained in the 1971 State School Facilities Survey. The Cuba Landing Elementary School cafeteria was thirty yards from the school building, thus forcing children to brave inclement weather. It was also inadequate to serve 250 children. The survey recommended that the Landing build a new cafeteria.

Wheeler wanted to build a kitchen next to the gymnasium and to use part of the gym as a multipurpose room, but his plan stirred protest. People in the Landing wanted both their gym and a new cafeteria. To support their claims, they pointed to Clarksville's new cafeteria, which had been built without sacrificing the gym. The Landing would accept nothing but equity.

At the February 14, 1974, board of education meeting, Wheeler acknowledged the protests by Landing residents. "We talked about partitioning off the gym. Come to find out, people don't want that."

"Are you kidding? Phones are ringing all over the place," said the board member from Clarksville.

The board tried to reassure Landing residents by showing a delegation a gym and cafeteria combination in a neighboring school system, but the visitation did not still protests.

In March, 1974, Wheeler visited the Cuba Landing Parent-Teacher Association to explain the building program, and then addressed the regular meeting of the Cuba Landing City Council. He produced a blueprint of a multipurpose room for their perusal and explained, "All elementary schools [in the state] are that way. I'll guarantee you this gym can be cleared in twenty minutes. But if the people don't want to build this, I say let's drop it."

"I can't see why there would be any objection," said Mayor Robbins. A city employee agreed and commended Wheeler in his role as superintendent. "You've done ten times as much as was done in the fifty years before."

It looked as though Wheeler had eliminated opposition in the Landing until the Lions Club held a special meeting and voted unanimously against the plan. Since the Landing's Lions Club included among its members many of the town's merchants, politicians, religious leaders, and prominent citizens, it was a political force to be reckoned with. To ensure that the club's counsel was heeded, a Landing delegation composed of Lions Club members attended the board of education meeting of April 11, 1974. The delegation filled the meeting room, and Wheeler greeted them. "I really didn't expect such bitter opposition to the plan. Any time you're messing with school buildings, people get interested."

Wheeler reported that a state department of education official had visited the Landing earlier in the day and had said that the state would agree to either a multipurpose room or an adjoining building. An adjoining structure would cost an extra $50,000. "In analyzing the situation financially, we can afford it." (This statement was misquoted in the *Shiloh Crier* as "we can't afford it," and caused Wheeler grief at the May meeting of the Buck Snort Parent-Teacher Association.)

The chairman of the board sought to still a rumor that Clarksville received better treatment than the Landing:

> It wasn't with the idea that Clarksville would have a nicer cafeteria than the Landing. Back when Martin was superinten-

> dent, the state said we had to connect the buildings, but we didn't have enough money to pay the teachers, let alone build. Clarksville won't have anything nicer than this.

The chairman was seconded by Wheeler. "If anyone thinks we're balancing one community against another, they're dead wrong."

The chairman then asked the delegation, "You all think you can live with this building plan?"

The delegation could. Wheeler learned that Shiloh's communal frames of reference could countermand both state recommendations and board decisions. As Judge Henry said, the delegation taught Wheeler that "he has to work with them."

This knowledge came too late to influence Wheeler's behavior with regard to Buck Snort and its determination to remain a viable community. Residents wanted the Buck Snort school to remain open, but the state department of education had twice recommended consolidating Buck Snort with Clarksville. The board of education refused to do so: the two members from South Shiloh were effective lobbyists in this cause and, under the leadership of Wheeler, had petitioned for another state survey of school facilities. The 1971 survey acknowledged local desires by recommending that the Buck Snort school continue on an interim basis. Wheeler publicly said that the board had done all it could do – the Buck Snort school problem was caused by the state and the local board could not force the state to change its recommendations. He talked with pride of the 1971 recommendation: "It took a lot of politics to get that."

But more politics were involved than simply exchanges between the board and the state department of education. The threat of consolidation had led to the founding of the Buck Snort Parent-Teacher Association. Its members looked north and saw that the Landing and Clarksville schools were being remodeled and that a new high school was under construction. They understood that the changes in the schools were being touted as representative of developmental change in Shiloh. Referring to the crumbling school building in Buck Snort, they asked Judge Henry, "How do you think that makes [us] feel?"

It made South Shiloh residents determined to get a new school. The Buck Snort Parent-Teacher Association saw the 1971 recommendation as a poor suggestion, so it launched its own campaign under Tom Blaine, a political leader in the county.

Blaine approached the leader of the state's Democratic Party for help. The party leader wrote the elected Democratic state superintendent of schools on the matter and was informed that the new school could be built if the local board initiated the proper procedures. South Shiloh's own reckoning placed the blame for the problem on the local board, particularly on Wheeler, rather than on the state bureaucracy. The community wanted Wheeler to petition for a new school in South Shiloh. The conflict between Wheeler and local political leaders grew into a struggle for control on two fronts. Wheeler argued that exchanges between local schools and the state bureaucracy were his domain; his opponents disagreed. He also claimed control of local educational policy, but his opponents challenged him on that front as well. The only important question that remained was which side had the political power to force its view on the other.

These rival positions crystallized in the election campaign for county judge (see Chapter Two). Judge Bass sprinkled South Shiloh with signs reading, "The Judge is for a new school. Are you?" South Shiloh's magistrates discreetly contacted Wheeler about the matter. One said that he had talked with Wheeler privately because he did not want to involve the school in politics. Judge Bass snorted at this. "Hell. There's politics in everything. Even where you go to church."

The rival candidates were also busy. Henry and his supporter, Tom Blaine, visited homes in South Shiloh. When conversations turned to the school, frequent mention was made of the state superintendent's letter, Democratic Party influence on state decision making, and Henry's Democratic Party affiliation.

Shiloh's political activity in the election for county judge forced a public display of educational policy making. On August 9, 1973 the *Shiloh Crier* carried a front-page banner: "Board Plans New School." The story quoted Wheeler as saying that he had "spearheaded the drive" for the Buck Snort school. The board was unanimous on the subject: "It's a must for Shiloh County." The story ended with Wheeler's comment "that this project is solely the work of the Shiloh County Board of Education, with no political influence on the local level."

A copy of the newspaper appeared at the initial in-service workshop for the ES project. A teacher who was a lifelong resident with strong ties to Shiloh's political arenas read the story and said of Wheeler's closing statement, "You lie, Bill Wheeler."

Henry won the election. He and Blaine paid Wheeler a visit and showed him a copy of the state superintendent's letter. The politicians responded to Wheeler's concerns, saying, "We'll do the dirty work. Regulations can be broken, laws can be bent." All that was necessary was Wheeler's cooperation.

Blaine organized delegations to appear before the board to gain Wheeler's cooperation. One such delegation came to the October 1973 meeting. Wheeler greeted the group, declaring, "If any of you can get to the governor, I say get with it and go. It'll take political clout."

"If push comes to shove, will the board go to [the state capital] with us?" asked Blaine. The board agreed to do so.

"We'll do all that's necessary," said Blaine.

After the delegation left, Wheeler told the board, "Boys. We got a fight on this Buck Snort thing." Members of the board nodded their heads in agreement.

The matter of who had the political power to force his agenda on the schools came to a head, of sorts, when Judge Henry telephoned Wheeler about a minor problem. Wheeler exploded. "I told him it was none of his goddamn business . . . . I'll use them, but they won't use me."

By January 1974 the county's political leaders and Wheeler were at loggerheads. The political establishment concluded that the only way to get a new school, and thus to make good some campaign promises, was to force Wheeler's cooperation.

This effort began with another delegation visit to the board. Blaine said that Judge Henry was arranging a meeting with the state department of education at the state capital. Members of the board said they would attend, but care would have to be taken to protect Wheeler. "In his position, he can't go too strong. We don't want to put Bill on the spot because he has to work with the state officials."

Prior to the state meeting, the local board met with South Shiloh residents in the Buck Snort Elementary School. The meeting attracted nearly thirty adults and helped to distinguish three sets of attitudes: Buck Snort residents did not trust Wheeler; board members intended to keep the Buck Snort school in operation and to press for a new building; Wheeler maintained that he and the board had done all they could do. The issue of a new school would have to be settled by putting political pressure on the state department of education.

Wheeler opened the meeting with an explanation. "The basic problem is that the county schools are in a process of change. It seems like the people that's been left out is this particular attendance center." This was the fault of the state department of education because their "regulations have the force of law." The regulation governing the building of new schools required that a local board show an enrollment of at least 240 students. The Buck Snort Elementary School served 85 students in grades one through five, so the local board could not meet the state requirement.

A member of the audience asked about grades six through eight, which had been transferred to the middle school. "How many would you have if the grades you've taken away were here?" He was told 110.

A member of the audience said that there would be no problem with enrollment figures if Wheeler would redistrict school attendance areas. Wheeler cited attendance figures to show that this was impossible. "We've got 340 at Clarksville. We've got 250 at the Landing. We've got 85 here."

The board chairman sought to reassure the crowd. "They'll never close this as long as I'm chairman. I'm highly opposed to busing these little ones all the way to Clarksville. If we move this school away from here, the value of your property will go down. You'll lose the spirit of community."

Wheeler supported the chairman. "We're going to talk to the state superintendent. If that doesn't work, we'll try another route. What we are saying is we'll keep the school open. We'll try and build you a new one."

"What do you want us to do?" asked a member of the audience.

"I don't know. I think you're going to have to have faith in your board, faith in me," said Wheeler. But the audience was short on faith.

"Do you want to hear that if folks don't get a school out here, there'll be a rebellion? Well, I'm telling you," claimed a member of the audience.

"If you push and bring political power to bear, I'll go along with you," said Wheeler.

The meeting with the state department of education was held in March. Wheeler opened the meeting. "To say the state department of education hasn't worked with us would be a lie." Members of the delegation from South Shiloh later said that Wheeler's opening statement was the lie: he was saying one thing to the state and another thing to them.

When a member of the state department asked what people wanted, a mother said, "A new school. Just build one that won't fall down. This one is going to fall down."

The state superintendent wanted to know about finances and local opinion. "Have you got the money to build this kind of school?"

"I think we can bond it," Wheeler responded.

The state superintendent asked, "How's the board?"

"We're solid for it," replied the chairman.

But a larger problem affected the South Shiloh school. Over twenty school districts in the state wanted to build in defiance of state department of education recommendations. Should one be allowed to do so, there would be no valid reason for denying the others. The state superintendent asked, "Suppose we say no on this. What are you going to do?"

"Keep operating it," said the chairman. "I couldn't go along [with busing small children all the way to Clarksville]. It wouldn't be justice." Since the chairman had to recognize any motion before it could be acted upon, his statement carried weight.

The state superintendent and his staff left the room to discuss the matter. When they returned, they offered to allow the board to buy three or four relocatable classrooms (trailers or modular units) to replace the Buck Snort Elementary School and allow South Shiloh time to sustain a population growth that would guarantee state approval of a new building. As the state superintendent put it, "Let Judge Henry go steal some people from [a neighboring] county."

Renovation of the existing building was suggested as an alternate plan.

"As good as the other elementary schools?" asked a delegation member.

"No. We won't promise that. Really and truly, you just can't afford to build a $300,000, $400,000, or $500,000 school for eighty-five children. You're just not that rich," said an assistant superintendent. He pointed to population figures in Shiloh. "People are moving north."

"I dispute you on that," said the chairman.

The delegation brought up the question of redistricting Shiloh's school attendance areas. "If you want to start a fight, redistrict. You're fighting for your life and I hope you can live. But you can also tell these eighty-five they can go elsewhere. I think you've done a great job. We're not going to close your school," said an assistant superintendent.

The state superintendent again referred to population figures in South Shiloh. "The last six or seven years show no growth."

Without growth, there would be no school built in Buck Snort unless it was financially sound to do so. In recommending relocatable classrooms and renovation, the state superintendent said, "If the cost is prohibitive, then we'll reconsider. If it's going to cost almost as much as it would the other way, then I'm not in favor of it."

The formal meeting ended on this note, but its informal consequences were only beginning to be felt. Wheeler had taken no part in the debate. After the meeting, he told the board chairman, "There comes a point when you have to stop pushing."

"I didn't push hard enough," claimed the chairman.

The split between Wheeler and the chairman pleased Tom Blaine. On the trip back to Shiloh, Blaine said that Wheeler had told his chairman before the meeting that the meeting would be a waste of time; Shiloh would gain nothing from it. The chairman asked Blaine why Wheeler knew something that he did not. Information was not being shared as it should be. The incident eroded Wheeler's political support on the local board, and word spread that the chairman was not happy with Wheeler. "He wants to run things. We have to live here after he's gone," said the chairman to several teachers who were complaining of Wheeler's actions.

The Buck Snort school issue did not die with the state meeting. Wheeler attended a Buck Snort Parent-Teacher Association meeting in May, 1974. The audience continued to show their distrust of him. Asked what was being planned for their school, Wheeler said that it would be renovated and new floors, ceilings, and lights would be installed.

"Why can't we see what we're going to get?" asked a member of the audience.

"What do you want me to say I'll do?" asked Wheeler.

"When will it be done?" asked a member of the audience.

"This summer," said Wheeler.

"You're going to do it, but there is nothing definite about it," said a member of the audience.

Blaine remarked, "It would be so easy to make people in Buck Snort happy. We're almost to the point where we're ready to get down on our knees and start begging."

"I'm sorry I didn't satisfy you," said Wheeler.

"We didn't say you didn't – we said you could."

"I haven't given up on the idea of a new school yet," said Wheeler.

"I haven't either," said Blaine.

The conversation then turned to equity between communities. Reference was made to an article published in the *Shiloh Crier* on April 18, 1974, reporting that the board had approved plans for building a new cafeteria at Cuba Landing. The story had said that a planned alteration would cost $50,000 more than the original proposal and had misquoted Wheeler as saying, "Financially, we can't afford it." A member of the audience said, "I don't understand how twenty-seven people [i.e., the Cuba Landing delegation to the board on the night of the decision] could talk you out of $50,000 in one night."

"No. It wasn't that. Don't ever think that. I didn't back up," said Wheeler.

The conversation then shifted back to Buck Snort. A Methodist minister told Wheeler, "There is a credibility gap. You say something is going to be done, but where's the results?"

"I believe there is. I believe you're right," said Wheeler.

The next morning a reporter for the *Shiloh Crier* was contacted by Blaine and told that Wheeler had a news item about remodeling the Buck Snort Elementary School. The next edition of the *Crier* carried a story that said a new floor, new ceiling, and new lighting would be installed over the summer, and they were.

This did not end the issue. Blaine still insisted on a new school for Buck Snort. In his reckoning, the only obstacle in getting it was Wheeler. Given the disquiet in South Shiloh and Cuba Landing, the growing awareness of problems among school board members, and the attempts of teachers to form political alliances aimed at curbing Wheeler, that obstacle could ultimately be overcome.

As described earlier (see Chapter Three), Wheeler's actions set the stage for Shiloh's political processes. His attempts at imposing classroom change failed and led the teachers to reach outside the schools for political support in curbing what they saw as his abuse of power. They found plenty of support, for Wheeler had antagonized many people: the Band Boosters were not happy with his treatment of the band director; the Landing was not happy with his plans for their cafeteria; and South Shiloh saw Wheeler as the chief obstacle in getting a new school.

But, despite the many sources of opposition, in January 1975 the board of education voted four to one in favor of renewing Wheeler's four-year contract. However, the meaning of the vote was unclear. Counsel for the board said, "I suggest you might not put anything on record. As long as there's nothing on record, nothing's settled." Counsel's suggestion would leave the way clear to discuss salary.

"I think we're haggling," said a board member who supported Wheeler.

Wheeler agreed that his current salary was adequate. "What I need is official notification that you intend to hire me. That's what I need," said Wheeler.

"Intent for approval is what you're asking," said the chairman.

"We hired," said a board member.

"What you're doing is offering me a new contract. We'll wait on the salary," said Wheeler.

"The intent is not hiring him," said the chairman.

"Are you offering me a new contract?" asked Wheeler.

"Yeah," said a board member.

"You offered me a new contract," stated Wheeler, and the matter seemed settled. But after the meeting the chairman, who had voted in favor of the motion, insisted nothing had been decided. The board had not obligated itself and would not do so until the minutes of the meeting were read and approved.

In the meantime teachers, board members, and politicians agreed that Wheeler must go. In late January the chairman visited Wheeler at the board of education office.

"I don't know if you know why I'm here," said the chairman. Wheeler handed him a signed and dated letter of resignation.

At the next board meeting the minutes of the previous meeting, which included the vote to offer Wheeler a new contract, were approved as usual and there was no outward sign that anything of importance had occurred. Nevertheless, by this time the impending administrative change in Shiloh's schools was common news in the county.

The news was confirmed by Wheeler in a meeting with his principals, which was called in February to prepare the school system for an inspection by a federal review panel. The purpose of the panel's visit was to determine whether the Experimental Schools program was actually funding comprehensive educational change in Shiloh County, among other selected school districts. The panel's decision would determine whether ES would continue as an agency program.

"The rest of this project depends on you all. What you say to them will have something to do with the funding you get year after next," said Wheeler.

Wheeler had chosen the wrong group to spearhead the ES project in Shiloh. Not one principal supported the federal project. As they said:

> You have to have faith in the teacher. Leave her alone. Most elementary teachers are dedicated.
>
> I'm not responsible for the success of the federal project. At least I don't feel like I am. I'll just try to do the best job I can.
>
> I'd quit before I'd use the diagnostic notebook.
>
> Anybody that knows anything about schools knows that we don't know anything that will change everything.

In reaction to Wheeler's charge that continuation of the project depended on the principals, "It seems like he's trying to put it on us. But if Bill Wheeler, college consultants, and project coordinators can't do it, I don't see how we can come up with the answers."

The meeting ended with the appearance of the review panel. Wheeler greeted the panel by saying, "We've implemented comprehensive changes one through twelve. It's there. You'll see it. We could not have done this without extra funding from Experimental Schools."

"Will the change continue?" asked a panel member.

"They're a damn good staff. They'll continue," said Wheeler. His next remark indicated that he knew his attempts to change classroom behavior were a failure: "We may not have done anything here in Shiloh County. It may be an optical illusion."

The meeting broke up and the review panel ate lunch in the Clarksville school cafeteria. After lunch the panel returned to the board of education office to find a visiting industrial spokesman. "It looks like I set this up. But I didn't," said Wheeler.

The spokesman was effusive in his praise of the ES project in Shiloh under Wheeler's leadership. "I think the image of the schools in the last five years has completely changed. A lot of people are moving here that wouldn't have moved here five years ago," he said.

Wheeler again admitted failure. Not all of the changes he had imposed were going to continue. Individualized instruction was being abandoned in the high school because "students like to be in a group." As for the rest of the changes he had attempted, "I've got to believe it's successful or else it'll all come crashing down."

The review panel conducted a two-day inspection of the school system. Their report said it would be better to alter the name of the agency's program from Experimental Schools to Demonstration Schools. But the final decision was to continue the program.

The review panel's decision had no effect on events in the Shiloh school system. The major problem besetting board members was the choice of a new superintendent. The immediate goal was "to settle all of this" because of community reaction to rumors. "I've had over 400 phone calls," complained Wheeler.

At the March board meeting Wheeler announced, "I've signed a contract with another system, so I'll be leaving." He then turned to the reporters in attendance and said, "I do think we ought to get this worded right," and he helped them write their stories.

The board then discussed Wheeler's replacement. "I feel like we ought to stay in the system this time. My suggestion to the board would be Mr. Collins," said the chairman.

"Give him a two-year contract," suggested another board member.

"We've done a lot of thinking on it already. I got five phone calls last night. This thing is driving me crazy," said the chairman, pressing for a decision.

But the board came to no decision and this resulted in a special meeting on March 22, 1975. The chairman opened the meeting by saying:

> I'm sure you all know why we're here. Hopefully we can elect a superintendent. When we hired Bill we were entering our building program and we needed someone with experience along that line. Now it's our duty to protect it.
>
> If you've got a man eligible in the county, give him a chance. These boys have been with us so long, they deserve a chance. I've had controversy, both pro and con, about Mr. Collins. He said he would take it for two years. Within six to eight months, if any three board members feel he's not doing a good job, he'd step down. Collins is the oldest man. As a rule, seniority goes a long ways.

A second board member had his say. "As far as making a decision, I would have to go along with Collins." A third board member was "willing to go along with the consensus of the board. Whoever does get in there is going to have an awful lot of pressure on them because we can't let this system stop."

"My mind's been made up for several weeks. Once I make up my mind, I never change it. I'd be willing to give Mr. Collins an eight-year contract," said the fourth board member.

The fifth member called for an executive session at which he spoke his mind. "It looks like you guys have made up your minds. Why the rush? What the hell's the hurry?" He suggested appointing an interim superintendent for sixty to ninety days and continuing the search. "There are a good many options."

The chairman reported on Collins's reactions to the interim proposal. Collins had told the chairman that, "I don't see how I could establish myself. I don't believe it would be fair to me. Within six to eight months, if any three board members feel I'm not doing it, I'll step down."

Legal counsel also spoke against the interim superintendency, noting that state law allowed an interim appointment only if death removed the office holder. The dissident board member decided to accept the majority opinion. "I'm going to vote whatever you all vote. I'm not going to have a split board," he said.

The chairman then said, "We've got to settle down. We've got to get this system settled down. It's our duty to do so. We've got one of the finest systems, building-wise and programs. Now it's up to us to protect it. We can't afford to let down."

"We can wait until next December. But would it change things? The board has made up its mind," said another board member.

"Let's go vote," said the onetime dissident. The board returned to the public meeting.

"Gentlemen. We've met. No further discussion. I'd like to have a motion to appoint Mr. Collins as superintendent," said the chairman. The motion was made, seconded, and approved five to zero.

"You've made a good decision," said Wheeler.

The next order of business was Wheeler's request for permission to apply to a new federal program that offered money to sustain exemplary school programs. The new program would continue much of what ES had begun.

"Another $200? That's how we got in this damn mess to begin with," protested a board member, referring to Wheeler's initial ES application. The board agreed it was time to "settle down," rather than embark on another cycle of imposed change. This meeting marked the end of the strategy of forming systemic linkages between Shiloh's schools and external agencies in order to fund change.

The board's new priorities were echoed throughout the system. In the August, 1975, meeting of the board of education, an assistant superintendent explained the financial status of Shiloh's ES project:

> In the next year's budget we've got to pick up about $35,000 in Experimental School expenses. We've got this for the next two years to be faced with. After this project is over, we're supposed to pick up these programs. I'm sure we can't.

A board member wanted to know how the school system could afford the $35,000 to support the ES project. "We haven't got that much," said the assistant superintendent. Programs would have to be dropped.

The board did not attempt to resolve the issue of what programs would be dropped. But the trend toward rejecting imposed change was made clear in a message that Collins sent to all teachers prior to a one-week in-service workshop held in late August 1975. The message read, in part:

> The Shiloh County School System has a contractual obligation to fulfill with the N.I.E. [National Institute of Education]. I trust that each of you will be most understanding and have the "patience of Job" in seeing the Experimental School Project to a successful conclusion. I request your cooperation and your sincere effort in the task we have before us.

Wheeler's demands for change had been replaced by Collins's requests for patience. In fact, the only reason the ES project was not jettisoned entirely was that Collins did not wish to incur local criticism. "They'd say Wheeler got the money and I let it go." Collins would not run that gauntlet.

Collins made certain, however, that he was personally disassociated from any further ES-inspired demands for educational change. When Wheeler had been superintendent, his authority had supported the ES project and the project coordinators. Collins abandoned both in an address to his teachers during an in-service workshop. "Any good system has to have people helping you," he said, and the people charged with the responsibility for bringing the ES project to a successful conclusion were the two project coordinators. Without the superintendent's authority to make them a powerful political force in the school system, the project coordinators once again became adjunct personnel. Shiloh's political processes had severed the systemic linkage between the county's schools and national educational policy.

The eulogy for Shiloh's ES project was delivered by Drs. Jones and Lampkin. The project coordinators had arranged for the consultants to address teachers during the first two days of the August 1975 workshop. Dr. Jones spoke on the first day, giving an overview of the entire project. He told of being approached by Wheeler to write the original letter of interest. This was "a crash effort. We had ten days to make a decision. The thing in that proposal was that it did focus an effort by an entire district to change teacher behavior."

Systemwide individualization was a difficult goal. "It would be tremendous, theoretically, if you and I could function as physicians. Our problem is, unlike a physician that treats a single illness, we treat an entire child. No one can teach you how to do this because no one knows how." But the attempt to do so was significant. Dr. Jones had talked to ES staff members in Washington. "Without diagnostic instruction, this project would never have been funded."

The effort to implement this new mode of instruction had led to a case of system shock. "You started off with a crash and you've been crashing ever since. Some of you know what the hell we're talking about, and some of you never will."

Dr. Jones later summed up his perspective of the entire effort to impose change on Shiloh's classrooms. "Bill Wheeler was the project," and now Bill Wheeler was gone.

The second day featured Dr. Lampkin. He also talked about individualized instruction, but from a philosophical perspective:

> Everybody talks about it. Many of you have been doing it for years. Individualizing is really a philosophy of education. You have to believe in two things: one is that a student can learn; the other is that learning is an active process. If you're sensitive to the fact that every student in here can learn and it's up to you to find the materials that will allow it, then you have individualized.

Shiloh's teachers were not taken with such graceful philosophical exposition. They had resisted the pressure to change under circumstances unfavorable to their cause; now circumstances favored them. Wheeler was gone and Collins was under a mandate to "get this system settled down." The teachers exercised full and undisputed control over their classrooms; they were under no compulsion to change, and they would not.

The schools were more relaxed in the fall of 1975, as Mr. Season observed in his last visit to Shiloh. After visiting several classrooms, he said that he could see no evidence that attempts to change teacher behavior had been made. Teachers were using textbooks to give group assignments and were relying on lectures to disseminate information. A project coordinator agreed with Mr. Season. "The schools have gone to sleep."

The project coordinator was only partially correct. The schools had "gone to sleep" with respect to the federal project, but they were responding to community agendas for developmental change. Both Judge Henry and Tom Blaine had committed themselves to getting a new elementary school for South Shiloh, and their local political futures hinged, in part, on fulfilling that pledge. Their political commitments also led them to oppose Wheeler's reappointment and to support Collins's application. They saw Collins as a man with whom the court house politicians could work in meeting community priorities.

The opportunity to meet South Shiloh's demands for a new school came during the state's general elections. Both Judge Henry and Tom Blaine had risen to positions of power in the state's Democratic machine. When invited to meet with the Democratic candidates prior to the election, they impressed Dr. Kay, the candidate for state superintendent of schools, with South Shiloh's need for a new elementary school.

Henry and Blaine continued to press their case after Dr. Kay's election victory. Dr. Kay had been a local school superintendent prior to election and told news reporters that he had "the viewpoint from the local school district. I think I know what's on the minds of many people." Dr. Kay said that he planned to take a hard look at the size of the state's consolidated schools. He wondered if they were becoming too big and eliminating close contact between teacher and student. "Perhaps we are losing something that a modern building cannot replace."

Blaine made photocopies of this news article, underlined appropriate passages, and mailed the copies to all school board officials. The political climate now favored South Shiloh's agenda for developmental change in the schools.

To make certain the opportunity would not be missed, Blaine led a South Shiloh delegation to a meeting of the Shiloh County Board of Education immediately after Dr. Kay took office. "The county judge and I had a chance to talk with Dr. Kay," Blaine explained. "He wouldn't make any promises, but said 'come and see me.' His philosophy while he's up there will be to let school boards make these decisions."

Collins doubted that campaign rhetoric would affect the workings of the state's educational bureaucracy. He told the delegation, "I'm just like you all. You can have hope." But unlike Wheeler, Collins was willing to cooperate with Henry and Blaine. "I'm sure that no harm can come in scheduling a meeting with Dr. Kay," Collins said.

The discussion turned to population figures and to the fact that, while the state's policy had been to limit new school construction to attendance areas with at least 240 students, the Buck Snort Elementary school had 88 students enrolled.

"Would you say we're wasting our time to go down there with 88 kids?" asked a member of the delegation.

"We can try and hope," said Collins.

"We're just kidding ourselves. Go down there with 88 kids? There's no way," said another delegation member.

"I think it's going to take a little politicking. Politicians have a way of doing things that sometimes overrides policy," Collins remarked.

"We've got everything in the world against us," said Blaine – except the knowledge that Dr. Kay was sympathetic toward South Shiloh's application. The board petitioned for a new state survey of school facilities and for a public hearing with the survey team.

The survey team visited Shiloh in late May 1976 and held a public hearing in the new high school. The meeting was attended by about seventy-five people, including county politicians and the board's legal counsel. The chairman of the board called the meeting to order and explained to the survey team, "I think this group here is interested in a request we have for a new structure in the southern end of our county."

Collins took the floor to explain the purpose and format of the meeting to the audience:

> Every five years there's a facilities survey team that visits the county. These gentlemen are not here to debate us tonight. In

> the past the state department of education [has required] around 240 students for new construction. We're hoping we can kind of find some way to change these guidelines.

The chairman of the board made a suggestion that would change the state department's guidelines. "What I'm trying to get the survey team to see is the way to judge Shiloh County [as] exceptional." He pointed out that there was population growth in the northern part of Shiloh and the additional children were going to crowd existing buildings. The solution was to build a new elementary school in the southern part of the county and alter attendance districts. "We want to build a modern, permanent brick school out there. You don't build a school for today. You build it for the future."

And the future held promise of even more industrial development and population growth for Shiloh. "There's no end to construction in Shiloh County, way I see it," said the chairman. But growth attracted people whose children needed adequate schools. As the chairman said of Shiloh's last industrial boom, "They woke us up when they moved in on us last time."

The Clarksville board member supported the chairman. Plans were underway for construction of a hydroelectric plant in his district. The plant "is going to employ 200 people: They're going to have children. We have to bleed them off somewhere." The new school was the only answer. "We don't have the room at Clarksville. We'll have children on the stage again."

A board member from South Shiloh spoke in favor of the school. "These people . . . want a school out there and they deserve it. We all have old rules for building, but I feel there are times we have to change."

The county's political leaders expressed their support. "On behalf of the people we make rules and regulations that sometimes do not fit every case," said Blaine. He urged that an exception be made to the 240-student policy.

The county sheriff also favored a new school. "We've got the money. If there was ever a need for a school in that area, it's now. These are young people here. They're going to raise kids. We've got to get schools for them."

Judge Henry summed up the local perspective:

> We see progress in every area of Shiloh County. People in the southern part of the county feel like they've been left out.

> And they have. They've said they did not want to be treated like the back end. I have people in the Landing tell me it's a shame that people in the southern part of the county can't have a decent elementary school. All of the people respectfully request that you allow a school in the southern part of the county.

The survey team wanted to know about the school district's bonding power. The assistant superintendent in charge of finances said, "I don't think it would be a problem as far as financing [is concerned]."

The spokesman for the survey team then told the audience of his team's purpose and function:

> We're fact finders. We do the legwork for the cabinet. Our recommendations will depend on what we hear tonight. The main thing is not to overbuild. The greatest thing is the number of students in the Buck Snort area.

"Have I missed anything?" the spokesman asked the other members of his team.

The spokesman had indeed missed the entire point of the meeting, from Shiloh's point of view. The board attorney brought Shiloh's priorities into perspective by asking what would happen if the team's recommendation did not meet with local approval. The survey team spokesman said that was up to the board. "They have sixty days to accept or reject," he said.

"Then the local board can make their own survey?" asked counsel.

"You will have to convince someone to change their mind," said the spokesman.

A lawsuit against the state department of education could do that.

"If we butt head on," replied the spokesman. "You've got a perfect right to get another survey from some other source. But your best bet is negotiations. I'll assure you of this: we'll give you every consideration we can."

After the meeting had ended, the chairman of the board of education offered another solution to the enrollment problem: "We'll redistrict until we get [the school] built and then we'll take them where we want."

The state later sent a representative to Shiloh to make its recommendations public at an open meeting of the Shiloh County Board of Education. The state called for a new elementary school to be built "no further south than the Pickering Road." The Pickering Road was a mile and a half north of Buck Snort's traditional community boundary.

"This is pretty much what we've been pulling for. But the site might have to be shifted around," said the chairman.

"We simply locate it in a general area," said the state representative.

"This is going to cause a sensation through the back end of our county," said the chairman.

The meeting ended. Since the county had gained state approval for a new elementary school, but not in the desired location, the recommendation was challenged. In the August 1976 meeting of the school board, Buck Snort fielded another delegation. "How obligated are we to go to the spot the state picked?" asked a delegation member.

"The state will have to approve the site. They won't let us issue the bonds," replied Collins. But there was a chance that local political initiative could alter the state's recommendation.

"This is something we've been fighting for for ten or fifteen years," said the chairman. "I was disappointed in the location. I asked if they couldn't be a little more optional on the spot. They said something could be worked out."

"That's just not far enough back for the southern part of the county," said a delegation member.

An alternative site was mentioned. The survey recommended that the school be placed "no further south than the Pickering Road," but the county might negotiate to locate it two miles further south, which would be within Buck Snort's traditional community boundaries. "Buck Snort's losing a school, but it's staying in the community," said a delegation member of the alternative site. The board thus gained community approval for the location of the new school.

The Shiloh County Board of Education negotiated with the state department of education for a revised recommendation. Rather than "no further south than the Pickering Road," the new recommendation read "in the vicinity of the Pickering Road." Two miles further south was interpreted to be "in the vicinity," and that was where the school was placed – in the northeastern section of the Buck Snort community.

Part 3

Analysis and Conclusions

7

Persistence and Change in Shiloh

The focus of this volume has been the manner in which Shiloh's towns, governments, and schools have made political decisions to use external resources in meeting local needs. Shiloh determined its own fate by both mobilizing internal social and political resources and manipulating external agencies to advance local programs. The story of developmental change in Shiloh County thus sheds light on the nature of the systemic linkages – what Loomis considered the articulations that allow two social systems to be thought of as one unit[1] – between local and extralocal institutions.

TWO PERSPECTIVES ON CHANGE IN SHILOH COUNTY

Much of the literature on rural North American communities, as well as the literature on developmental change, assumes that the systemic linkages between rural institutions and national bureaucracies are controlled at the national level; that is, federal programs have a predictable impact on developmental change in rural areas. This impact hypothesis posits extralocal decision making as an independent variable and local events as dependent variables. The hypothesis was first popularized by the anthropologists Vidich and Bensman. Their report on Springdale, New York, described a rural community dominated by the agencies and culture of mass institutions. In their view, Springdale was as much a possession of national bureaucracy as was Kropa, Yugoslavia, or the American colony of Palau in the Western Carolines.[2] They encouraged students of rural communities to "study the community within the framework of large-scale bureaucratic mass society rather than as the polar opposite of urban society."[3]

Vidich and Bensman document the impact hypothesis with an anecdote about the modernization of Springdale's telephone company. Their initial information indicated that the decision to modernize was a local choice. Further investigation showed, however, that local management was opposed to modernization but did not have the political power to counteract the dictates of extralocal decision makers: "Not only were state agencies, other bureaucracies, and a whole range of experts decisive in the case of the telephone company but similar connections and influences were at work in politics, education, religion, and the cultural life of the community."[4]

The impact hypothesis underlies the rationale, theory, and practice of conventional developmental change. Another anthropologist, Edward Spicer, described the rationale for imposed programs of developmental change: "The inconsistencies and the low level, or lack, of linkages among the cultures and institutions of modern states cause one segment within the whole to seek changes in the way of life of other segments."[5] But it was a political scientist, Edward Weidner, who characterized the use of the impact hypothesis in programs of developmental change most sharply:

> The developmental strategies of governments, universities, business organizations, and other associations are the principal independent variables . . . . Different kinds of development – economic, social, political, technological – are the ultimate dependent variables.[6]

The impact theorists ignore the possibility that local political processes can control developmental change. The local control or local autonomy hypothesis posits local political processes as independent variables, with developmental changes as the dependent variables, or at least as variables that can stay the impacts of imposed programs by intervening between systemic linkages and local institutions.

John Bennett's observations of local autonomy led him to suggest that rural communities seeking developmental changes have either created new institutions or modified older ones to "manipulate and control" external agencies.[7] Some of this manipulation is focused on local control of living links so that governmental policy and bureaucratic programs can be modified to fit local contexts.[8]

The "relationships between local units and urban-based organizations are subject to constant readjustments," a process in which local political autonomy is a force to be reckoned with at the highest levels of government.[9] As Bennett phrases the local view of these relationships:

> the external system takes on some of the characteristics of a powerful card player, who has the stakes but who is not always attentive to the game, nor even particularly concerned about winning – only about following the rules. Hence, if one knows the rules, the big player can be manipulated into . . . providing resources.[10]

Bennett documents the local autonomy hypothesis with an anecdote about local political processes intervening in graze land lease policy in Saskatchewan, Canada. An administration that favored large ranchers was defeated at the polls by a party pledged to more equitable leasing. The new policy lasted until the large ranchers formed a political alliance with the early beneficiaries of equitable leasing and lobbied the provincial government "to leave the land situation alone and not to press for further redistribution."[11] Here local political autonomy influenced policy, systemic linkages, and policy implementation.

The local autonomy hypothesis has gained support in recent years, particularly from an interdisciplinary group of scholars that met in 1973 to discuss developmental change and concluded that the impact hypothesis was:

> if not irrelevant, then less relevant as a model for explaining development and, in particular, for explaining the failure of development programs. The participants were in fact searching for an alternative approach, which came to be called "development from below."[12]

Shiloh is an exemplar of development from below, and therein lies the explanation not only for its successes in promoting programs of developmental change, but also for its successful resistance to imposed programs of change.

Shiloh's record fully supports the local autonomy hypothesis. The county entered the 1960s as a small, rural, political subdivision with an agricultural economy whose residents wanted developmental change in order to stem the tide of emigration. This desire for change was transmitted to Shiloh's elected leaders as a mandate for action.

Shiloh's history of developmental change began when influential men from prominent Cuba Landing families formed a political alliance with other small communities to lobby the state legislature for the right to issue municipal industrial bonds. The lobbying was successful, and the Cuba Landing City Council used its new legal right by issuing $50 million worth of bonds to entice a metal-processing plant to construct a facility nearby. This was followed by additional bond issues in a period of rapid and massive industrialization, giving the county nearly $300 million worth of industrial facilities. In 1970 the county had 2,203 industrial jobs.

The immediate result of this industrialization was that Shiloh's institutions were overwhelmed by the sudden growth in population and did not have the revenue to meet new demands. In this sense, Shiloh's experience corresponded to the normal tendency of rural industrialization "to exacerbate the very conditions it was supposed to have relieved" because of payroll leakage, small multiplier effects, and "the inability of local governments to convert growth in the private sector into public revenue."[13]

Responding to the overcrowded conditions in the schools, the Shiloh County Fiscal Court made the $150 million bond issue for the construction of a metal-processing and metal fabrication complex contingent upon an in-lieu-of-taxes agreement between industry and the schools. Industry agreed to this. Then the state legislature passed a bill enabling local school districts to impose higher property, franchise, and utilities use taxes. The fiscal court imposed all three taxes on behalf of the schools – despite lobbying efforts by industry and powerful state politicians.

Local autonomy was also apparent in the fiscal court's actions concerning the Home Rule legislation. Since the attainment of statehood, the state constitution had defined its policy toward local political subdivisions in restrictive terms: local political subdivisions had only those rights specifically granted to them by the state legislature. The Home Rule legislation reversed this policy by granting local political subdivisions all legal rights not specifically reserved for state and federal governments. One of these new rights was the privilege of imposing a payroll tax. Given this opportunity, and an impending election that could be swayed by the imposition of the payroll tax, the fiscal court levied the tax.

The exercise of local autonomy in the schools was a little more complex. Superintendent Martin entered the 1970-71 school year with new sources of income, a countywide consensus on the need for developmental change in the school system, and no clear local priorities. His successor, Superintendent Wheeler, accepted the recommendations of an independent school survey as a plan for action. Wheeler quickly renovated and built additions on older buildings and opened a new consolidated high school. He also forced the retirement of older teachers, raised beginning teachers' salaries, and enticed younger teachers with better credentials into the schools. Local demands for change in the schools appeared to have been met.

An analysis of this period would indicate that the local autonomy hypothesis appeared to become subordinate to the impact hypothesis. Wheeler gained support for an Experimental Schools project, planned new instructional programs, and imposed his plan on Shiloh's schools. At the same time, he became embroiled in local political processes as Cuba Landing protested his plans for a new multipurpose room and South Shiloh demanded equity in educational facilities. The contest between local priorities for developmental change and Wheeler's imposed programs seemed to be settled in favor of the latter when the Shiloh County Board of Education appeared to offer Wheeler a new contract. But this was not the case. The news of the contract offer simply strengthened political opposition to Wheeler, led to his forced resignation, and severed the systemic linkages between the federal Experimental Schools program and the county school system. Local autonomy once again held sway.

Local autonomy also held sway in the South Shiloh Elementary School issue. For many years the state department of education had recommended consolidating the Buck Snort and Clarksville Elementary Schools. However, South Shiloh residents had no intention of losing their elementary school. Henry won the election for county judge in part because he agreed to pressure Wheeler and the state department of education on South Shiloh's behalf. Through some adroit political plays, including the forced resignation of Wheeler, Henry and Blaine first won the school and then helped place it in the proper community location. Once again, Shiloh's political processes controlled the course of developmental change.

LASTING CHANGE

One final task remains — explaining why locally generated programs of developmental change are effective while imposed programs apparently have few if any lasting consequences. Shiloh's successes in both promoting local programs of developmental change and resisting imposed programs of change can be understood in light of some social science perspectives on values and acculturation.

Lionberger, a rural sociologist, made an observation that helps put Shiloh's values in perspective:

> Values may be regarded as importance ratings which people attach to things, conditions, and circumstances. They may also be regarded as goal objects to which people orient their thinking, actions, and feelings. As such, they become important organizing themes in the behavior of individuals.[14]

An examination of Shiloh's record in developmental change reveals a dual value/goal orientation which crystallized into three political strategies. First, Shiloh modified local institutions to forge systemic linkages between the county and external policies and programs. The goal here was to use external resources to meet local priorities. Some examples of this political strategy include the use of municipal bonds to industrialize; the school system's imposition of higher property tax rates, franchise, and utilities use taxes; the fiscal court's imposition of a payroll tax; the fiscal court's initiatives in gaining adequate ambulance services, in seeking external funds to renovate the court house, and in providing recreational facilities; and the securing of funds to participate in the Experimental Schools program.

Second, a tendency toward localism is manifested in political strategy in Shiloh. From the time of its incorporation as a political subdivision, Shiloh's communal frames of reference – from family to county – have demanded individualized political attention. Under the influence of localism, for example, South Shiloh's fiscal court magistrates demanded that county-generated funds, such as payroll tax monies, be diverted to road improvements in South Shiloh; the Cuba Landing City Council and the Clarksville-based Shiloh County Chamber of Commerce demanded magisterial redistricting so that their communities would receive an increased share of payroll tax funds; Buck Snort retained a post office; South Shiloh gained a new elementary school; and Cuba Landing rejected Wheeler's plans for a multipurpose gymnasium.

Local domination of Shiloh's institutions also led to a third political strategy, the use of local political power to control the course of developmental change by influencing the living links in systemic linkages. This strategy was illustrated at the county level when the fiscal court intervened in the metal-processing firm's plans for purchasing pollution control equipment and when the fiscal court met the Supreme Court's one-man, one-vote ruling in magisterial redistricting. Another illustration is the way in which the county limited the geographical sway of the planning and zoning commission and made certain that the commission's rulings would be subject to local approval.

The third strategy was based on the adroit use of communication networks and political tactics to consolidate Shiloh's disparate communal frames of reference into one: the county as community. In the beginning stage the informal communication networks were used to spread derogatory gossip about Shiloh's leaders, as illustrated by the teachers' reaction to Wheeler's imposition of the Experimental Schools program, and by organized religion's threat to publish the petition that would force a vote on the county's policy of prohibiting the sale of alcohol. In the second stage social boundaries were solidified and sanctions imposed by means of social shunning. This was illustrated by the churching of a South Shiloh resident and by the teachers' silent opposition to Wheeler and his consultants in the dispute over diagnostic instruction. Shiloh's communal frames of reference did not embrace profanators or men advocating fundamental changes in the classroom.

Spicer has observed that the social structure of contact between groups is an important determinant of cultural change. His proposition:

> directs attention to the nature of the social relations through which contact is maintained and suggests that they have a determinable influence on the character of the innovations offered, on the acceptance and diffusion of these, and on the modification of these innovations. . . . No change sequence can be explained without some consideration of the nature of the social structure.[15]

In Shiloh's case, key determinants of change are the links and the nature of their proposed innovations.

The best illustration in Shiloh of the workings of Spicer's proposition is the contrast between the approaches taken by two living links, Judge Henry and Bill Wheeler, in advocating change. Judge Henry sought to achieve consensus by allowing people to influence decisions. Judge Henry chose this approach because he knew that

Shiloh demanded that its leaders act as common men. As one of Shiloh's political leaders explained, "You get to thinking you're bigger than the people, they'll put the axe to you – real quick." Judge Henry's successful election campaign focused on door-to-door contact with voters in which he presented himself as a common man concerned with Shiloh's lack of developmental change. He consolidated the local sources of power and influence by nullifying the Cuba Landing community bloc vote; by gaining support in his extensive familial group; by gaining support from familial groups in South Shiloh, using the social ties of South Shiloh's leading politician, Tom Blaine; and by agreeing to support South Shiloh's bid for a new school. In office Judge Henry always sought consensus in advocating change. He made frequent use of open meetings to consult with the public and explain his programs. His presentation of himself as a common man, coupled with his skill as a living link to the resources of external agencies gave him secure office.

Wheeler's style of advocacy was quite different. He first tried the common-man approach and then abandoned it, instead controlling events by planning for people rather than with them. Wheeler's view was, "One man's got to do it."

This style of advocacy made Wheeler the living link in the social and political relations surrounding developmental change in the schools. In his successful efforts to meet the recommendations of the independent school survey, Wheeler made decisions and the school board approved them. When he sought to link his schools with Washington's Experimental Schools program, Wheeler used the approach of planning for people throughout, first by enlisting consultant expertise to produce what was supposed to be a locally generated letter of interest, and then by using consultant expertise to manipulate community-school dialogue during planning.

Washington's objection to Wheeler's use of consultants in planning actually strengthened his position as a living link. Instead of hiring a competent, full-time consultant to produce a usable plan, Wheeler controlled the piecemeal contributions of various consultants. His role as living link was enhanced when his plan was funded and again when Mr. Season asked permission to show Shiloh's schools to a federal review panel as evidence of the program's success. "They're really begging, aren't they? I've beat them," said Wheeler.

Eventually Wheeler lost control of the social and political relationships in the schools because of the nature of both his own behavior and the federal program. Wheeler's Experimental Schools project was based on the premise that the teachers' professional performance was inadequate. His plan for improving their performance was to use federal funds to buy materials and to hire consultants who would train the teachers to alter their classroom behavior. Wheeler would then use the authority of his office to enforce cooperation among the teachers. His assault on their professional role met with resistance for two reasons. First, the teachers viewed his intrusion into their classrooms as an abuse of administrative authority. Second, they felt that the change from traditional class instruction to individualized instruction would lessen their own authority as teachers and thereby diminish student learning.

But it was Wheeler's insensitivity to Shiloh's communal frames of reference that finally determined the course of developmental change in the schools. After assuming the superintendency he forced the older teachers without credentials to resign. These teachers were all native to the county and had their own political constituencies in Shiloh's families, neighborhoods, churches, and communities. The forced resignations marked the beginning of Wheeler's social and political isolation. As Shiloh's residents said, "We take care of our own."

An anonymous telephone call from a "concerned citizen" expressed the teachers' unhappiness. Another incident involved malicious gossip about Wheeler that was transmitted by a teacher into the informal communication network.

The board of education rejected Wheeler's recommendation to fire the band director because the board members understood that the Band Boosters had consolidated Shiloh's communal frames of reference into a powerful political base, one that would oppose the band director's removal. Local political domination of the board was used to curb Wheeler.

When Wheeler's plans for building collided with community priorities in Cuba Landing, the plans were changed. And when Tom Blaine and Judge Henry placed the blame on Wheeler for South Shiloh's lack of a new elementary school, Wheeler was faced with political opposition capable of consolidating countywide support. The teachers soon joined this opposing group and used the communication networks and political tactics to build a political climate that would force the board of education to oust Wheeler. The opposition was successful because Wheeler's style of advocacy had led to a decline in board support for his initiatives.

Wheeler's behavior as a living link largely determined the fate of Shiloh's Experimental Schools project. Without the advocacy approach that Wheeler used to obtain ES funding, plan educational change, and force its implementation, the program fell into a political vacuum. Although Shiloh's ES project was less successful than originally hoped for, the school system itself was a success. All of the recommendations of the independent school survey, save for the elimination of an elementary school in South Shiloh, were met. Comparing Shiloh's schools with those of a neighboring urban school system, one of Wheeler's critics admitted, "They haven't got a thing to match this. But Shiloh County isn't used to Bill Wheeler's kind of leadership."

Cultural change is determined not only by the nature of the social structure and the behavior of those who introduce change, but also by the nature of the innovations themselves. Here, too, are clear distinctions between the programs of developmental change promoted by local interests and those imposed by external agencies. However, in both types of developmental change, the innovations are either accepted, rejected, or given new meanings that allow them to be integrated into traditional practices. This process is what Herskovits calls "syncretism."[16]

When locally promoted programs of change occur, as they did in Shiloh, the innovations are either additions, or are syncretized to become additions, to preexisting facilities, services, or practices, and the innovations are rationalized as being in the best interests of the community. When programs of developmental change are imposed by external agencies, as was also the case in Shiloh, the innovations are replacements of preexisting facilities, services, or practices and cannot be syncretized because they are rationalized as being in the best interests of the donor group, not the receiving group.

Judge Henry's programs of developmental change were responsive to local demands and provided changes that were either additions to facilities, services, and practices or were syncretized and rationalized as such. His programs were thus accepted. Wheeler, however, was responsive to the recommendations of the independent school survey as well as to local demands for change. Where he implemented changes that Shiloh saw as additions in the county's best interests (such as renovating older buildings, adding to existing structures, and building a new consolidated high school), his actions were supported. Where proposed changes conflicted with local interests, the changes were redirected. And where Wheeler was incapable of meeting demands for additional facilities, as in the case of the South Shiloh Elementary School, his efforts were rejected and support sought elsewhere.

Wheeler's problems in introducing change were compounded when Shiloh was selected for participation in the Experimental Schools program. The ES program that Wheeler planned and implemented was responsive to national educational policy, not to local demands for educational change. Furthermore, his innovations did not add to Shiloh's traditions of teaching; instead they were intended to replace classroom practices. Teachers and students therefore rejected his innovations, and the rejection left Shiloh's Experimental Schools project without an effective living link because the county's commitment to the program was legalistic and not – as in the case of a school for South Shiloh – communal.

The disparity between donor and receiver interests in imposed programs of developmental change may be inevitable. Spicer and Pitt agree that imposed developmental change is a consequence of ethnocentric tendencies in the donor group.[17] Bennett has carried his analysis further, arguing that national institutions are of a standard bureaucratic type, governed by overt policies that are universal (equally applicable in all cases) and lawful (formulated by legislatures or accredited administrations and sanctioned in law).[18] Rural actions are guided by values of individualism, egalitarianism, and particularism. When the two traditions meet at the local level, as they did with Shiloh's Experimental Schools project, overt bureaucratic policies are either syncretized or rejected, thus allowing for the persistence of local behaviors in the face of external pressures for change.

Schultze recommended that the federal government embark "on a program of social experimentation" to learn how to change local institutions.[19] But if Shiloh's experience is any guide, it appears that such federal intervention will not change local institutions in a fundamental way because they will remain responsive to contextual variables traditionally beyond the grasp of national policymakers. At best, all that national programs of developmental change can hope to achieve is the funding of locally acceptable additions to facilities, services, and practices. However tempting it is for federal policymakers and program implementors to think in terms of replacing fundamental individual and institutional behavior at the local level, they need to acknowledge that local political decision makers often have the expertise to manipulate or evade external pressures for change. Such expertise guarantees that local institutions, such as Shiloh's schools, will persist despite federal pressures for institutional modification.

Notes

1. Loomis, *Social Systems,* p. 33.
2. Arthur J. Vidich and Joseph Bensman, *Small Town in Mass Society: Class, Power, and Religion in a Rural Community* (Princeton, N.J.: Princeton University Press, 1968), p. 432.
3. Ibid., p. vii.
4. Ibid., pp. 386-387.
5. Edward H. Spicer, "Developmental Change and Cultural Integration," in *Perspectives on Developmental Change,* ed. Art Gallaher, Jr., p. 172.
6. Edward Weidner, "Developmental Change and the Social Sciences: Conclusion" in *Perspectives on Developmental Change,* ed. Art Gallaher, Jr., p. 240.
7. Bennett, "Microcosm-Macrocosm Relationships," p. 442.
8. Ibid., pp. 446-448.
9. Ibid., p. 443.
10. Ibid., pp. 450-451.
11. Ibid., p. 448.
12. Pitt, *Development from Below,* p. 4.
13. Summers, "Small Towns Beware," p. 20.
14. Lionberger, *Adoption of New Ideas and Practices,* pp. 92-93.
15. Edward H. Spicer, "Social Structure and Cultural Process in Yaqui Religious Acculturation," *The American Anthropologist* Vol. 60, p. 433.
16. Melville J. Herskovits, *Man and His Works* (New York: Alfred Knopf, 1960), p. 553.
17. Spicer, "Developmental Change and Cultural Integration," p. 172; Pitt, *Development from Below,* p. 4.
18. Bennett, "Microcosm-Macrocosm Relationships," pp. 445-448.
19. Schultze et al., *Setting National Priorities,* pp. 462-463.

A Methodological Postscript

As part of the formal arrangement between Shiloh's schools and the Experimental Schools program, the Shiloh County school system agreed to serve as a research site for Abt Associates Inc.'s Project Rural, a five-year, multidisciplinary research effort focused on the relationships between communities and schools during a time of planning and implementing educational change. The Shiloh superintendent accepted this provision, and in late 1972 Ronald P. Estes, Jr., took residence in Shiloh as an on-site researcher, where he remained until his death in the winter of 1973. Dr. Robert Herriott, director of Abt Associates Inc.'s Project Rural asked me to take Mr. Estes' place. I agreed to do so.

My late entry into the project created one drawback. The contract between Abt Associates Inc. and the federal Experimental Schools program stipulated that raw field notes were the property of the on-site researcher. Mrs. Estes was reluctant to share her husband's field notes, and thus primary verbal and observational data concerning much of Shiloh's planning were not available to me.

Even with a late start, however, I had the promise of better than four years of data collection and writing. Given the extraordinary length of field time, I concluded that the most sensible research strategy would be a natural history approach. My first task was to become acquainted with Shiloh, its major internal subdivisions, and the goals that the communities were using as agendas for action. The second task was to frequent the arenas where those mandates for action were forcing decisions. The third task was to keep close watch on how and why decisions were being made. The long, slow, and sure natural history approach was adopted as a research strategy that allowed Shiloh's events to delineate the important matters.

Fieldwork lasted from April 1973 until June 1975. What was my place in Shiloh during that time? Nonexistent in the county's family units, marginal in its communities, nominal in religious life, but fully integrated into Shiloh's political affairs. Given that Shiloh's political decision making was the focus of research, my integration was appropriate to my task.

Data Collection

A source of data was secondary materials. These included historical accounts on file in various Shiloh locations, such as county, city, and school records, as well as the morgue of the *Shiloh Crier;* historical documents on file in various state university collections; historical accounts on file in the State Department of Education; contemporary accounts on file in various state and federal offices; regional newspapers; national news sources; and the *Congressional Record.*

Collection of data from primary sources was limited by techniques of observation, participation, and direct and indirect interviewing. I assumed the observer's stance during regular attendance at the Cuba Landing Methodist Sunday Church services; the Cuba Landing and Clarksville City Council meetings; the Shiloh County Chamber of Commerce meetings; the Shiloh County Planning and Zoning Commission meetings; the Shiloh County Fiscal Court's regular and specially called meetings; and the Shiloh County School Board's regular, special, and executive meetings.

While I took no formal notes during the Cuba Landing Methodist Church services, for each of the other organizations I used notebooks reserved exclusively for recording formal deliberations. The notebooks were as complete as possible but were not verbatim transcripts.

Participation in Shiloh was not confined to my research activities. My family was invited to one family reunion and to several family celebrations, although we were not related to anyone in Shiloh County. My wife, Pat, and I participated in a large number of community events, including public and private gatherings, as a couple. Pat also participated in the Cuba Landing Women's Club and the Shiloh Homemaker's group. In addition to familial participation in Shiloh's events, I also participated in Operation Helping Hand, a volunteer relief effort to help the victims of a tornado; the Shiloh County Historical Society; the Clarksville Lions Club, the Cuba Landing Lions Club, the Shiloh County Bicentennial Committee; the Shiloh County Chamber of Commerce; and the meeting between Superintendent Wheeler, the Shiloh County Board of Education, the State Department of Education, and the delegation from South Shiloh petitioning for a new elementary school.

Interviewing complemented the data gathered through participation and observation. Formal interviews were a minor part of data gathering because of my commitment to a natural history approach. The major source of interview data was informal interviewing – conversations with individuals eliciting their perceptions of current events and decisions, but there were times when formal interviews could not be avoided. One of these occurred when Project Rural's Community Change Study needed information about Shiloh's churches. The survey forms were taken to Shiloh's clergymen, and the required information was secured – but at a cost – because some of the clergymen were not pleased with survey research techniques and resented outsiders' prying into church affairs. In another attempt at formal interviewing, I furnished Wheeler's project coordinators with a set of questions about planning. The coordinators discussed the questions and their answers and arrived at what they considered reasonable answers. Wheeler responded to the same set of questions and his answers were congruent with his coordinators' responses. The problem was that other, less structured, responses from Wheeler, his coordinators, and other well-informed sources did not support what was said in formal interviews.

The net result of formal interviewing was that people supplied the answers they wanted publicly known. This conclusion was supported by Wheeler. When he learned of a prospective directed interview with a community member, Wheeler said, "Hell. He'll just lie to you." Wheeler's comment was consistent with his own approach to interviews and contained at least a symbolic truth about the credibility of data generated through this technique.

My doubts about responses to formal interviewing are perhaps attributable to the natural history approach that I had selected as much as to conclusions about the responses themselves. Whatever the reason, I placed more faith in informal interviews. Many of these were conversations with people who had a vested interest in community agendas. These people were most willing to discuss what they wanted, how they were going to get what they wanted, and what the major obstacles were. Since I deliberately interviewed individuals representing all sides of any major issue, the triangulation of conflicting positions served to minimize error from any one data source.

The data recording for the indirect interviews differed from what followed in both observational reporting and formal interviewing. Rather than record conversations on the spot, I recorded informal interviews after the conversations were over. After-the-fact recording led to data loss, but those memorable insights that people have about the contexts of their endeavors were retained. There is no way to calculate how many interviews took place. Given the natural history approach and the reliance on conversations as research sources, parts of nearly every social exchange became data.

Major Strategies Used in Gathering Data

I approach fieldwork as a game of strategy. Games of strategy have goals and rules of play. My goal during fieldwork was to glean relevant information. The rules governing fieldwork are set by the research population, which determines what can and cannot be probed. My fieldwork strategy is that of data maximization. Rather than relying on one individual or group, I deliberately seek out multiple sources of information and thereby minimize particularistic biases.

My strategy led to three different fieldworker postures in Shiloh County. The first posture was that of the traditional neutral observer. I used this stance in recording formal sessions, such as city council meetings or in-service teaching workshops. I simply joined the people present at these gatherings and recorded all the information I could. Gradually, I was accepted as an odd sort of reporter whose stories were never printed in local or regional presses, and I was accorded fellowship by media reporters who wondered why I continued to write after they had stopped.

I was privy to information about decision making, but rarely responded to questions about what those decisions meant in Shiloh's terms. To do so would violate some informal agreements I had with decision makers about untimely dissemination. Violation would ensure that further information would not be forthcoming, and my goal was to maximize information, not to minimize it.

I departed from the neutral observer stance several times. For example, when Wheeler and the board of education were meeting with the first delegation from South Shiloh (see Chapter Six), Wheeler asked that the board go into executive session with the delegation and that the room be cleared of all people who didn't have immediate business. The news media and several interested spectators left the room. Wheeler then said that I, too, should leave. I said that the Shiloh County Board of Education had signed a contract with the Experimental Schools program that ensured my access to any and all school business. Since school business was to be discussed in the executive session, I refused to leave.

My refusal to leave the meeting opened up new sources of information. No longer dependent upon Wheeler's perceptions about South Shiloh's demands for educational equity, I was also privy to community perceptions. Also, from that point on executive sessions remained open to me.

Another consequence of the incident was ironic. Ethnographers are fond of portraying themselves as friends of their research subjects. By refusing to leave the executive session, I appeared to be making enemies of Wheeler and the board, an impression that potentially allied me with dissident community groups. There is thus another dictum to be added to the folklore of fieldwork: the best information may come from friends, but there are times when the appearance of making the right enemies guarantees a wider network of information.

The second major posture I assumed in gathering primary data was the interested party. I talked with people about their perceptions. This was a pleasant way to gather data because the conversations followed whatever subject the respondent wanted to discuss. I learned about tobacco planting, soybean prices, familial concerns, cave exploring, student perceptions, and Shiloh's traditional territorial rivalries. Most of these conversations were partially recorded and later transcribed and placed in chronological logs.

The third posture was that of a polite but persistent interviewer. I would tell the individual I wanted to interview that I already knew about the subject under discussion and was only interested in the individual's perceptions to make sure the record was complete. The first time this posture was used was after Henry and Blaine visited Wheeler about the South Shiloh school (see Chapter Six). Henry was basing his South Shiloh campaign on a pledge to secure the school. Blaine was supporting Henry and was showing the letter from the State Superintendent of Schools to the head of the state's Democratic Party as proof that a county judge with Democratic Party connections could get the school built.

Wheeler was less than overjoyed at the visit and complained to me about political interference in his schools. He identified Henry as a meeting participant, but he would not identify the third person in the discussion.

I brought the matter up with Henry. He was willing to talk about the incident in private and invited my family to his house. Several hours were spent there discussing the background of the South Shiloh effort and the incident in Wheeler's office. But Henry would not identify the third person taking part in the conversation in Wheeler's office.

I returned to Wheeler and told him about my conversation with Henry and then pressed him for the name of the third person in the exchange. Wheeler finally said Blaine had also been part of the meeting.

Assembling the Data

Observations of what does, in fact, occur in Shiloh were congruent with people's conceptions of what ought to be and how their county actually behaves. Every major agenda item in Shiloh became a political problem that was dealt with through political processes. It made no difference whether the observational data were gathered in formal meetings or in informal visitations.

Using observational data as a check on verbal statements is an example of triangulation, an elementary way of using different data sources to arrive at an understanding of a group's normal way of behaving. The goal is to use internal consistency to winnow out idiosyncratic responses so that the observer is left with data that reflect both the normal way of behaving and the culturally acceptable variations to the norm. These two bodies of data then become the basis for an ethnographic account through the process of pyramiding. In pyramiding data the ethnographer follows the lawyer's tactic of presenting masses of data, none of which is conclusive in itself, but which are overwhelming in the aggregate. That is what I have attempted to do in this volume with data from Shiloh's politics of developmental change.

I did not limit triangulation and pyramiding to primary data. I also used the perceptions of other observers as an independent check. The accounts in the *Shiloh Crier* were useful here, especially when the issues led to explosive encounters or when scheduling conflicts precluded my attendance at a meeting. Two major cases in point were Harold's meeting with the Clarksville City Council and the *Crier's* use of college journalism students to fathom Shiloh's Experimental Schools project. In both cases, I used the perceptions of independent observers to check the accuracy of my data. There was considerable congruency.

There was another check on the data's integrity. Project Rural followed a nonformative stance in its research and refused to share data with local officials. During the spring of 1974 Wheeler was concerned about Project Rural's data-gathering activities. Not only was Abt Associates Inc. sending questionnaires to teachers and county residents, I was attending supposedly private sessions between Wheeler and community advocacy groups. Wheeler was interested in what was being learned and where the information was coming from.

He distributed a questionnaire to all teaching and administrative personnel within Shiloh's schools. The questionnaire asked whether I had visited the respondent's classrooms and talked with the respondent, whether the conversations were positive or negative, whether the conversations disturbed the classrooms or teaching, and whether Project Rural was getting a "true picture" of Shiloh County and its educational program. Wheeler concluded, "Feedback from a questionnaire has indicated that the on-site representative has established an excellent rapport with the community and staff." I think Wheeler's conclusion was accurate; had a similar questionnaire been circulated through Shiloh's decision makers, the result would have been an even higher rate of positive response.

MY PLACE IN SHILOH COUNTY

Save for one crucial dimension, my family and I were marginal residents in Shiloh. We had no kinship ties in the county, we were not part of a neighborhood, our religious affiliation was tenuous, and we had only a minor place in a community. However, I was better integrated into the decision-making arenas of the county than most residents, and county decision making was the focus of my fieldwork.

We were outside Shiloh's family units because we were not related to anyone in Shiloh. Although invited to a number of family functions, my family and I were guests and not full-fledged participants. The account of Shiloh's familialism is thus gleaned from conversations with people firmly embedded among kinsmen.

My family and I were also insignificant in Shiloh's neighborhood groups because of lack of local ties. In the beginning we lived in a new apartment complex near the high school. The apartments were inhabited by people new to the county and without an understanding of the county's social organization. The county's communal frames of reference excluded the people in the apartments. "They don't belong to anything," was the way a Methodist minister phrased local perceptions of the people in the apartments.

We bought a house in Cuba Landing during the second phase of community integration. Within the immediate neighborhood were five households whose members were part of one extended family. Initially we did not fit in the neighborhood, but our daughter's attempts to join neighborhood play groups broke some barriers. We were accorded marginal standing in the neighborhood as play groups congregated first in one yard and then in another.

At the same time, I rented an office in Clarksville and took part in the daily gatherings in Clarksville's restaurants. My presence was tolerated in the lunch groups, but I was never fully integrated because of a lack of local credentials and the lingering suspicion that I was some sort of federal spy.

We were a nominal part of Shiloh's religious life because we attended both the Clarksville and Cuba Landing Methodist Churches on an irregular basis. Church attendance was due to research priorities, a desire to belong to something, and to enroll Laura in Sunday School. Laura's Sunday School exposure was necessary; she needed the company of her peers and the training in acceptable school behavior that Sunday School provides.

My marginal position in the county's social networks was transferred to my position among Shiloh's teachers. In the beginning, since I was without local ties, I was not significant in teacher reckoning – I was simply an onerous part of Wheeler's federal project.

By the spring of 1974 I was at least tolerated in the schools, and the teachers came to expect my presence in classrooms and in-service workshops, as part of faculty lounge conversations, and as a spy taking notes on conversations. Then Wheeler circulated his questionnaire.

Wheeler's questionnaire did for me what I could not do for myself. By the spring of 1974 the teachers were seeking allies in their struggle to oust Wheeler. The teachers thought that Wheeler's purpose in distributing the questionnaire was to use the questionnaire results to force me from Shiloh. Their perception may have been accurate, because one of the questions that Wheeler continually asked me through the winter, spring, and summer of 1974 was, "How do you get rid of an OSR [on-site researcher]?" The teachers were aware of Wheeler's stance toward me and thus saw me as a possible ally. This prompted them to do something unprecedented: They answered Wheeler's questionnaire truthfully.

Just as the teachers' political reckonings finally yielded me a place in the schools, my interest in Shiloh's political decision making yielded me a place in the county's decision-making arenas. As a neutral observer and interested party, I became both a potential resource and repository. The county made use of me as a resource when the *Crier* published parts of Shiloh's history long before the Historical Society published the full report. The *Crier* and Radio Station Clarksville also interviewed me several times, and the *Crier* published several of my photographs of newsworthy events. In return, the staffs of the *Crier* and Radio Station Clarksville shared a number of community understandings with me.

Entry into Shiloh's political arenas provided moments of personal gratification. Judge Henry sought my advice when Clarksville's businessmen pressured him to build a new court house. I counseled him to save the old building, which he did. In one of my last conversations as a fieldworker in Shiloh, Judge Henry asked me to speak at the dedication of the court house complex along with Shiloh's United States Congressional Representative, the state's two United States senators, the Chief Justice of the State Supreme Court and the Governor.

So, while my place in Shiloh was nonexistent in the county's family units, marginal in its communities, and nominal in its religious life, I was fully integrated into Shiloh's political affairs. Given that Shiloh's political decision making was the focus of research, my integration was appropriate to my task.

Index